DOJO WISDOM FOR MOTHERS

Jennifer Lawler is a writer and martial arts expert. She has taught writing and literature at the University of Kansas and she is the co-chair of the Book Division of the National Writers Union. She speaks frequently on writing, martial arts, relationships, work-life balance, parenting, and other personal growth issues. The author of more than twenty books, including *Dojo Wisdom,* which won an Outstanding Book Award from the American Society of Journalists and Authors in 2004, and *Dojo Wisdom for Writers,* her articles have appeared in *Family Circle, American Fitness, New Living,* and other magazines. She is a second-degree black belt in Tae Kwon Do and she has taught the martial arts and self-defense for many years. She lives in Lawrence, Kansas, with her daughter.

Dojo Wisdom for Mothers

100 Simple Ways
to Become a Calmer, Happier,
More Loving Parent

Jennifer Lawler

PENGUIN COMPASS

PENGUIN COMPASS
Published by the Penguin Group
Penguin Group (USA) Inc., 375 Hudson Street,
New York, New York 10014, U.S.A.
Penguin Group (Canada), 10 Alcorn Avenue, Toronto, Ontario, Canada M4V 3B2
(a division of Pearson Penguin Canada Inc.)
Penguin Books Ltd, 80 Strand, London WC2R 0RL, England
Penguin Ireland, 25 St. Stephen's Green, Dublin 2, Ireland
(a division of Penguin Books Ltd)
Penguin Group (Australia), 250 Camberwell Road, Camberwell, Victoria 3124, Australia
(a division of Pearson Australia Group Pty Ltd)
Penguin Books India Pvt Ltd, 11 Community Centre, Panchsheel Park,
New Delhi - 110 017, India
Penguin Group (NZ), cnr Airborne and Rosedale Roads, Albany, Auckland 1310,
New Zealand (a division of Pearson New Zealand Ltd)
Penguin Books (South Africa) (Pty) Ltd, 24 Sturdee Avenue, Rosebank,
Johannesburg 2196, South Africa

Penguin Books Ltd, Registered Offices:
80 Strand, London WC2R 0RL, England

First published in Penguin Books 2005

1 3 5 7 9 10 8 6 4 2

LIBRARY OF CONGRESS CATALOGING-IN-PUBLICATION DATA
Lawler, Jennifer, 1965–
Dojo wisdom for mothers : 100 simple ways to become a calmer,
happier, more loving parent / Jennifer Lawler.
p. cm.
ISBN 0-14-219634-7
1. Martial arts. 2. Parenting. I. Title.
GV1101.L387 2005
796.8—dc22 2004056541

Printed in the United States of America
Set in Guardi
Designed by Sabrina Bowers

For my mother, for obvious reasons.
And for my daughter, ditto.

In memory of

Chantal E. Anderson
(1978–2003)

Acknowledgments

I have to thank my editor, Lucia Watson, for everything from suggesting brilliant ways to make my books better to holding my hand through the production process. I also owe a debt of gratitude to my publicist, Acadia Wallace, for all her help in promoting my books. My agent, Carol Susan Roth, continues to guide and inspire me. What serendipity that she found me when she did!

Vickie Anderson should be recognized for her part in keeping my office running despite the interference of dogs and Jessica's best efforts to convince her to play games instead of work.

My writing colleagues and friends in the NWU, ASJA, FLX and every other organization I'm part of deserve a big hug for supporting everything I do (at least everything I do that they know about) and for always sending such warm and positive energy my way.

My martial arts instructors, Masters Donald and Susan Booth and Grandmaster Woo Jin Jung, deserve recognition for starting me along the way.

My daughter gets special credit for inspiring me every day. Without her chanting, "Get out of bed, you sleepy head!" at least once a morning shortly before dawn, I might never get anything done.

Contents

Introduction

When I first became a martial artist, it was because I wanted to lose weight and get into shape. Training in Tae Kwon Do seemed a lot more interesting than taking an aerobics class. It occurred to me that learning martial arts would also teach me some self-defense skills that might come in handy since I was a single graduate student who lived alone in not your best section of town.

I did not know that training would change my life—or as I always tell people, *save* my life. Training gave me discipline and structure, focus and perseverance, and a feeling of fearlessness. I started teaching martial arts and self-defense instead of becoming an English professor as planned. Which just goes to show, you never know what the universe has up its sleeve.

Almost immediately, I saw that the wisdom of the martial arts could be applied to everyday life. When I had trouble with a course in graduate school, the focus and perseverance I learned in martial arts helped me succeed. When I was afraid of a new challenge, such as taking the comprehensive examination for my PhD or writing my first book, my martial arts training saw me through.

I was not the only one to see these benefits. The martial artists all around me knew that they were leading better, more fulfilling lives because of their training. Often we would articulate what these principles were and how they worked in our lives. Many of us researched the history of martial arts to see how these connections and stories had been used by the generations before us. I interviewed many, many martial artists who shared their wisdom with me and told how they used it in their lives. When I first began training, people would ask me, "Wow, have you ever had to use your martial arts?" I always said, "No." I assumed they were asking "Have you ever had to defend yourself against an attacker?" and I had not. But after some years of training, I began answering the question this way: "Yes. I use my martial arts training every day of my life."

My belief in the power of martial arts to see me through was tested when my daughter, Jessica, was born. She has a rare genetic disorder called tuberous sclerosis. When she was just three days old, a medical resident told me, "Your daughter's brain is massively deformed."

That was not in the plan. The plan was, I'd have a wonderful little girl, pursue a writing career, maybe have a wonderful little boy in a couple of years, and create a pleasant home in our comfortable house on the right side of town. My husband and I would show the world to our children, become doting and generous grandparents as we grew older, and retire to Aruba. It was a nice plan, if I do say so myself.

But within a few years, I was divorced, supporting my disabled child on the precarious income of a freelance writer and living on the wrong side of town. Again and again, I relied on my martial arts training and the lessons I had learned not just to survive but to thrive. Now I have a wonderful career, an adorable daughter, and two comic dogs. I have devoted friends, and good relations with my parents and siblings. I have everything I want in my life, and nothing I don't. And I credit martial arts for giving me the sense to see this and the skills to get here.

My training helped me become a patient, focused mother, able to determine her priorities and stick to them. It helped me accept—embrace—Jessica's differences and to appreciate the joy she brings into my life. Because I know how much the wisdom of the martial arts has helped me as a mother, I have made it a point to share the principles with others. In the original *Dojo Wisdom* book and in my talks to groups around the country, I show people how they can apply the lessons of the martial arts to their lives even if they never step on the mat and learn to block a punch. People from all walks of life have told me they often read and re-read the book to get centered and to feel calmer and more inspired when they're getting a little burned out and fatigued. That's exactly what I hoped would happen.

Mothers have told me that they feel more focused in their mothering roles when they begin to use the *Dojo Wisdom* principles, and much less concerned with pressures and opinions of other people. Other mothers discovered the principles themselves before I came along and found that using the principles made them more confident in their mothering and helped them stay in charge. They tell me that they would otherwise have had much more difficulty raising their children to be happy, healthy adults.

When I began researching for this book by asking mothers across the country to tell me the guiding philosophy behind their mothering or the one piece of advice they'd give another mother, I was surprised at the sheer variety of the responses. They ranged from everything from "make sleep a priority for you and your children" to "you can't make your child different." But all of the pieces of wisdom I collected shared certain basic themes: You do know what you're doing. Stay in charge. Give yourself a break. And I realized that if a mother followed these basic ideas, she could deal with problems including crying and tantrums, sleep difficulties, misbehavior and discipline, giving attention and dealing with anger and frustration.

I have to admit that I am not always a perfect model of the principles I share in the book. There are indeed days when an observer would think that not only had I never heard of Lesson #21 (Practice patience as your child masters new skills), but that someone really ought to sit me down and explain it to me. Never mind that I wrote it myself. Rest assured that when I fail miserably, my daughter promptly reports me to the authorities—my own mother and father. Their job is to offer cookies and sympathy and listen to me defend myself.

The point, of course, is that while you'll be a calmer, happier, more loving mother by practicing these lessons, no one (least of all me) expects that you'll manage beautifully and effortlessly twenty-four hours a day, seven days a week for as long as someone in your life still calls you "Mom."

Of the challenges you face as a mother, the first one begins when, in the words of developmental psychologist Sandra Scarr, "A healthy newborn has been delivered in a more or less satisfying fashion. The baby is feeding well, has short nails and a clean bottom, and has not drowned. What now?"

The one hundred lessons in *Dojo Wisdom for Mothers* are meant to help you answer that question. The book doesn't advise you about when immunizations are due or propound the superiority of breast-feeding over formula feeding. What it does is help you shape a parenting philosophy so that you can be prepared to respond to challenges in a calm and clearheaded way, so that you can be consistent in how you treat your child (predictability is important to children) and so that you can make mothering choices according to your personal beliefs, priorities and goals.

The principles can be used to help you balance the demands of child-rearing and having a personal life, whether you choose to work outside the home or not. They help you become more focused, more effective and happier. They show you ways to keep your life calm and centered. They are not intended to become yet another thing on your to-do list to worry about, but instead, are meant to offer strategies for coping with the challenges you face. *Dojo Wisdom for Mothers* is about reducing the amount of stress in your life, not adding to it. I hope you find these lessons supportive and inspiring, as they are intended to be.

When I began training in the martial arts, I learned to say the phrase "Pilsung!" at certain points during training. I thought it meant something along the lines of "Good afternoon." Later, I learned it meant "Certain Victory!" At first, I liked "Good afternoon" better. It seemed quite a bit less—well, triumphant. But over time I learned to use the lessons of the martial arts to live like a warrior—courageously and fearlessly. I discovered that I could be a calm, joyful, loving parent, and that I could be a happy mother, regardless of circumstances, if I just loved my daughter and raised her the best I could.

So in the end I finally understood that "Pilsung!" does mean "Certain Victory!" and that it's a phrase worth saying when things look difficult or you're not sure you have the creativity to face up to this week's challenges. You do. You will.

Pilsung!

Dojo Wisdom
for Mothers

1

Seek a teacher

When I became pregnant, I looked around for help understanding what to expect. While I enjoyed reading books about pregnancy, I found it even more helpful to talk to people who had been through it—a childbirth educator, my friends who have children, my own mother. I realized that I needed a teacher, just as I had when I began training in the martial arts.

While you can read about martial arts techniques and watch videos of them, you need the support, encouragement and feedback that a real teacher provides. But the teacher who is right for you is not necessarily the teacher who is right for me. And the teacher who is most obvious (i.e., the one down the street from your house) or most popular (i.e., the one with the most students) may not be the right one, either. I know a terrific martial arts instructor who needs a wheelchair. I know another who is blind. They would not necessarily be obvious choices to teach martial arts, but they are well respected and highly regarded.

Once my daughter was born, I needed more guidance than ever. Sometimes I thought this might be because my daughter had special needs, but I soon realized that every new mother needs a teacher. Journalist Pamela Patrick Novotny writes, "The first time many women hold their tiny babies, they are apt to feel as clumsy and incompetent as any man. The difference is our culture tells them they're not supposed to feel that way."

To make the transition from clumsy to skilled and from

incompetent to competent, it helps to find a reliable teacher. That mentor won't necessarily appear miraculously (although that would be nice).

It will probably be up to you to find that mentor. Some of the teachers you find may be fairly obvious—a helpful health care provider can play one teaching role; mothers of slightly older children can play another. Your mother, a sister or friend with children of any age may be able to support and encourage you and help you problem-solve, even if you're facing a difficulty—sleeping or feeding problems, for example—they have not personally faced. They can still help you brainstorm strategies or describe how they coped with similar problems. It's best to find someone who's mothering style is compatible with yours and who has a similar child-rearing philosophy. Sure, there's something to be said about knowing what *not* to do, but most of us want a more positive, inspiring mentor.

Some of the teachers you may find won't be so obvious. For instance, maybe one of your friends is a dad who seems to have a parenting philosophy that matches yours and would make a good mentor. No one said your teacher had to be female! Or it could even be someone who has no experience with children. One of my colleagues has helped her best friend raise a daughter, although my colleague doesn't have children of her own.

One of my childless friends responded to my complaints of frustration by suggesting that I give Jessica more responsibility for self-care—a terrific idea that helped Jessica realize she could do more than she thought she could, plus reduced some of my stress because I wasn't constantly jumping up to attend to one of Jessica's needs. Early on, my daughter's speech therapist—who has considerable experience with special-needs children, and who is kind and compassionate to boot—became one of my very best teachers.

Finding a teacher will help you navigate the course. While each of us has a different mothering experience, sharing our knowledge and being open to learning from others can make us more effective, more confident mothers.

Exercise

Seek out a teacher who will help you cope with mothering tasks, challenges and concerns. While there are many good books on child care and mothering, you need to have a real live advisor— someone you can call up late at night for advice and commiseration. It might be your mother or a sister or a friend who knows the ropes. Don't expect to find this person in the obvious place and don't give up if you can't find someone right away. Create opportunities to find these teachers by joining mothers' groups, going where mothers are (the park, PTA meetings), letting others know you need help and advice and being open to finding a teacher in an unexpected place.

2

From your chi flows your energy for calm parenting

Martial artists recognize the importance of chi (also *ki* or *qi*) in their training. They learn to tap into their chi to perform arduous tasks. They also use a physical expression of the chi—the *kiai* or *kihop,* which is the martial arts shout—to help them generate the energy they need to defeat an opponent and to focus their energy on succeeding at a difficult challenge. Many people think of chi as simply your inner energy and focus, but it is also the source of creative energy. If you can tap into your chi, you can find the energy to create art, solve problems and respond to troubled times calmly.

As a mother, you need to be able to tap into your chi to handle the pressures of child-rearing—and there will be many, from getting your child to sleep through the night to teaching your teenager to drive. But your chi is not an endless pool. You have to replenish it. Those things that replenish your chi are just what you're most likely to be short on—sleep, time for yourself, nutritious food, physical exercise, emotional support. Yet it's important to renew your chi energy, so it's worth the effort of making time for what you need.

Like any parent, I have those times when I'm short-tempered, easily overwhelmed and frustrated instead of calm, in control and accepting. Instead of blaming my feelings on my mood, I recognize them for what they are: symptoms that I need to take better care of myself. When I find myself having to count to ten a lot, that's my signal that it's time to replenish my chi. I'll arrange for someone to watch Jessica so I can meet a friend at a coffee shop, or I'll make it a priority to get sleep on a night when Jessica is with her father. A year or two ago, I made a promise to myself that at least once a week I would go out with friends—for dinner, a movie, a cup of coffee—when I realized that I was always either working or taking care of Jessica and rarely spent time relaxing with people who are important to me. This new "rule" has helped me replenish my energy every week.

You need to take care of yourself in order to be a calm, responsive parent. It is not self-indulgent or selfish of you to take time for yourself. Although you may want to spend all the time you can with your baby when you're a new mother, or all your spare moments with your teenager before she goes off to college, you need to remember to give yourself time for yourself. Replenishing your chi helps keep you ready for the challenges that will inevitably come.

What works for you as a nurturing activity may be different from what works for me. Maybe getting your hair and nails done is just the thing you need. Maybe setting aside time for yoga class is essential. Maybe it's watching monster truck shows. Make it a practice to give yourself time for yourself.

3

Respect all mothering choices

"Who we are has been sidetracked by labels for who we aren't," writes Paula C. Howe, a family life educator. "Phrase names have divided us. Stay-at-home mom, new dad, parent of special needs child, working mother, job sharer, non-custodial parent, single parent, empty nester, spouse caring for spouse, parent with teens, teenage parent, elder caregiver—these and so many other titles have put us in little niches and kept us thinking that we can't help each other because . . . we are so different. But we are not a collection of separate sub-species. We caregivers are more like one another than not, no matter how we spend our days."

When you become a mother, it seems as though the choices you've made are suddenly held up for examination by everyone else in the world, even though your choices are made for the good of your family and yourself and for intensely private, personal reasons. No matter what choice you make—stay at home, continue with your career, work part-time or make some other flexible arrangement—someone is sure to criticize you or question you about it.

Instead of celebrating the diversity of choices mothers can make, we tend to criticize the choices other women make. Women who stay at home feel criticized for not contributing financially to their households. They may feel that others think they're too lazy or not intelligent enough to hold down a job outside the home. Women who work outside the home may feel criticized for not staying home with their children, as if they're selfish for the choice they've made. Even mothers who choose flexible work arrangements (part-time, telecommuting) in order to create balance in their lives may feel tension for not belonging firmly in either world.

No matter what choice you make as a mother, remember that you are worth defending. This is a principle that I often find I must teach to my martial arts/self-defense students. Many women come to me feeling as if they have no right to defend themselves—to protect themselves by physically stopping another person from harming them. They'll face a tiger for their children, but they somehow feel they aren't entitled to protect themselves with the same ferocity. As a teacher, my job is to encourage my students to see that they can stand up for themselves—and that they should. They learn to set boundaries, demand respect and feel stronger about the decisions they make, and in the end turn out to be much less likely to be bullied or attacked.

The same principle applies to the choices we make as mothers. You don't need to stand for people doubting, questioning or bullying you over your choices. This doesn't mean that you need to get into shouting matches with people who don't make the same decisions as you do. It does mean you can set boundaries and demand respect for what you do. If you stay at home with your children, you're not "just" a stay-at-home mom. If you have a job outside the home, you're not a selfish woman who puts her career before her kids. You've made the right choice for you—it's no one else's business.

It's important to respect the choices other mothers make, too. Just as you might have chosen to be a stay-at-home mother, your neighbor may have made a different choice. This doesn't make you a better mother—or her a better mother. By valuing all the choices that we can make, we do a lot to ensure that our sisters and our daughters can make the choices that are right for them. Embracing your own choice and the choices of women around you will help you become stronger and more confident yourself.

Often our negative reactions to other people's choices come from our own feelings of doubt or inadequacy. Very often the martial arts students I teach who feel they're not entitled to defend themselves actually don't want the responsibility. And some of them doubt that they can do the techniques effectively. But when they practice the techniques and learn to apply them, they realize that they can defend themselves, that they are able to take responsibility for defending themselves, and they have less doubt and more self-confidence in all areas of their life. In the same way, by fully embracing and respecting the different choices mothers make, you can move beyond your own feelings of doubt, uncertainty and defensiveness. Coming from a place of strength makes it much easier to ignore the criticizers and nay-sayers and to convince the important people in your life that you're doing the right thing.

Exercise

Respect the choices you've made as a mother—and respect the differing choices other mothers might make. Do what you must to make the right choice, but don't let other people's expectations affect you (well, your spouse's or partner's expectations need to be factored in, of course). Remember to be flexible: You may decide after your child is born that you want to stay home—or go back to work. And throughout your child's life you may make different choices. Many women change their work schedules when their children become teens in order to help guide them through this difficult period.

Make the right decision and respect it. Value the amazing range of opportunities and choices we have as mothers—and remember that you can always makes changes based on what you decide is important, what you need to do.

4

Be open to what happens next

A child learns and grows by being open to what happens next. They don't have preconceived ideas of what the world should be like. Martial artists are encouraged to adopt this childlike mind-set. The martial artist knows that if she's open, she'll grow in the art. When the teacher gives her a new challenge, she gives it a try. Although she might be involved in martial arts for the sport aspect or for self-defense, she is open to the other benefits the training brings her. When she works with a partner or competes in a tournament, she doesn't know how it will turn out but she's open to the experience.

As mothers, we sometimes think our children will grow up a certain way and that they'll follow a certain path. You may think your child should like classical music because you play the violin, or become a ballerina because you can afford the lessons that your parents never could. But of course our life with our children doesn't always turn out as planned. Instead of being upset or disappointed by this, we can be open to it and enjoy the new experiences our children bring us.

When my sister Bridget's third child, her only son, became interested in wrestling, she and her husband decided to support him, thinking he might soon tire of practicing several nights a week and participating in tournaments nearly every weekend throughout the season. But Patrick kept wrestling throughout grade school, middle school and now high school. Instead of finding all the time spent in the gym rooting for their son tedious or thinking how it prevented them from doing other hobbies and projects they might have liked, they embraced the experience, developed strong, lasting friendships with parents of other wrestlers and became involved in the organization that oversees wrestling in their area. Bridget has found that the experience has helped her stay close to her son and gives them a shared interest.

When some friends of mine had their first child, they were living in New York City, both with high-pressure jobs. They realized they wanted to be closer to their families and to raise their daughter in a more tranquil setting and to spend more time with her. Within a few months, they moved back to the Midwest—a move they hadn't expected to make before their daughter came along and reminded them of what was really important. Although the small town where they live now isn't anything like the vibrant city they left, they don't fret about it. They focus on the good things about where they are now, and they're open to where their children—now including a new son—might lead them in the future.

Exercise

Don't assume that your children have to follow in your footsteps or that you have to follow a certain path. Don't get caught up in planning their future for them—they'll have to figure that out for themselves. Let them discover what it is and show you. One mother I know who loves to sew frilly dresses and always wanted to see her daughter wear them had to resign herself when her daughter, then three, decided to wear camouflage pants and T-shirts every day for a year. Vickie wisely chose not to fight about it. And she remained open to letting her daughter pursue her own course. Vickie was not terribly surprised when her daughter rejected all of Vickie's interests (in interior design, fashion, flower arranging, history and art) and instead became a good athlete and eventually an athletic trainer.

As your children grow up, listen to them and their talk of the future. Do they really want to take piano lessons, or is that what you want for them? Maybe guitar lessons would be as good? Pay attention to what they like to do, and what they're good at.

In other words, let your children show you what their dreams are—be open to them—and don't decide ahead of time what your children and their lives should be like.

5.
Find your inner child

As parents, we often think that our job is to help our children develop control over their actions—to help them look without touching and to think before they speak and to weigh the consequences before acting. But by appreciating our children's impulses, enjoying their take on the world, and allowing them to sometimes lead the way, we can open up a joyful new world.

For mothers, deliberately cultivating your inner child—in martial arts, we call it the Beginner's Mind—helps you understand what your children are doing and why. It helps you appreciate their openness and flexibility. By remembering how new and amazing each experience was when you were a child, you can share in the joy your children have in exploring the world, rather than dismissing it or hurrying them along.

In martial arts, the Beginner's Mind is valued precisely because it is the beginner's. Beginning students are open to the information and experiences they encounter in the *dojo* (training hall). Because they don't know quite what to expect, they don't bring preconceived ideas and prejudices to their training. Like sponges, they soak up information and remain open and accepting.

As they progress in their training, their minds gradually become more closed. They understand that some ways of doing the front kick are better than others. They become more critical and demanding. While they're more accomplished as martial artists, they're also less open to new ideas and new ways of doing things.

Over time, the martial artist comes full circle. She begins to realize that her way is not the only way. She deliberately tries to cultivate a Beginner's Mind. In this way, she becomes accomplished *and* open.

If, as mothers, we can cultivate our inner child, keep our Beginner's Mind open, we can be competent and experienced adults who are also open to new experiences and delighted by ordinary, everyday events.

When Jessica and I took a trip to San Francisco, I thought climbing the steep hills would make walking tiring and bothersome, especially with a six-year-old in tow. (We live on the prairie, mind you, with very little exposure to hills of any sort.) When Jessica encountered her first hill, she immediately started running down it as fast as she could.

When I saw her charge down that hill, my initial reaction was to tell her to slow down and be careful. My second reaction was to keep a Beginner's Mind—and we ran down the hills together, laughing. This was certainly more fun than deciding the hills were tiring and bothersome. Later, Jessica had the good sense to convince me to ride the cable cars back *up* the hills. When I think back to our trip, I don't remember a single tiresome climb up or down any hills. Yet if I had had my own way, every single step would have been tedious. I'm glad I had enough sense to let Jessica lead the way. I'm also glad that these days my inner child isn't quite as hard to find as she used to be.

As I discovered, if instead of assuming your way is the best way, you can remain open to new ideas and new ways of doing things, you may be surprised at what your children can teach you.

Exercise

Consciously try to find your inner child and cultivate a Beginner's Mind. In a journal, write down how you felt the first time you tried something new—the first day of school, or the first time you tried to ride a bike, or the first time you flew in an airplane. Remember how scary and exciting it was? Wasn't it a good feeling to be scared and excited all at the same time? That's how it is for your children. Make a commitment to being open to those new experiences—and to experiencing old activities in a new way.

6
Identify and balance all of your roles

When a woman becomes a mother, it changes her perception of herself. She becomes bound up with her new child, absorbed and delighted. Sometimes being a mother is so consuming, you can forget that you play other roles as well. And sometimes the demands of your other roles—daughter, employee, wife—may make you feel you're not doing as good of a job in your mother role as you would like. But a well-rounded woman, a well-rounded mother, finds life a lot friendlier and more satisfying. U.S. Congresswoman Pat Schroeder was once asked, "How can you be both a lawmaker and a mother?" She answered, "I have a brain and a uterus and I use both." In other words, it's important to remember that there's more to you than being a mother.

In much the same way, the new martial artist may be taken with one of the aspects of martial arts training—practicing the beautiful forms, for example. Or, like me, focusing on sparring because it's so much fun. But a martial artist has to practice more than one aspect of the martial arts to be a true martial artist. She must try to master the techniques, and learn to perform the forms with agility and grace, and spar (or some form of *budokai*—the application of techniques). She must also try to adhere to character standards, being honest and courteous, persevering and kind. None of these is more important than another. Many new martial artists think the application of techniques—the sparring—is the most important thing because that's what they need to know to fend off a mugger. But that's not the most important thing. It's only one of many important things a martial artist learns, and if she focuses on only one aspect or another, she neglects the whole.

So in the same way, even though you may love being a mother and hate to spend a moment away from your kids (I know, I know: For some of us, this is an impossible state of mind to imagine), you do have other functions in life—maybe it's time to have a one-on-one with your sister or a friend you haven't seen in a while. Maybe the intellectual part of you needs a rainy Saturday afternoon at the library to catch up on what's happening in philosophy today. Maybe it's time for a date with your partner.

Identifying and balancing all of your roles means that you sleep better at night, feeling less stressed and pulled in all directions. You're more likely to get all of your needs met if you're willing to juggle the roles and pay attention to one today, another one tomorrow; one this morning and another one this evening. If you focus too much on only one or two roles, you can wind up feeling desperate, trapped and frustrated—not a good combination! So make an extra effort to decide which roles are most important to your life and well-being, and focus on taking care of those roles.

Exercise

Consider the various roles that you play. Make a list: mother, wife, volunteer, insurance agent. Then list the most important thing you can focus on in that category to make sure you're successful in the role. Everything will flow from that single message you tell yourself. You'll focus on the guiding principles for each of your roles.

For example, my roles and the guiding principles for each go something like this:

- Mother: provide loving attention to Jessica.
- Writer: show people how using the principles of martial arts can help them get what they want in life.
- Daughter: visit my parents twice a month with Jessica.
- Sister: acknowledge events in siblings' lives with calls, e-mails, cards, celebrations.
- Martial artist: expand and extend my martial arts knowledge and training.

As you can see, if I focus on one theme for each role, I can juggle multiple roles. I can easily decide if I'm making good choices and spending my time doing what I should be doing. If I tried to do too much in each role, I would probably feel overwhelmed. So focus on the most important goal or expectation for each role, and let that guide you as you balance your roles.

7

Push beyond your limits

For mothers, learning to push beyond your limits makes you more effective as a parent. You'll face this challenge when you first bring your child home and have to get up every two hours to feed her. And when your toddler's tantrums threaten to drive you bananas, you'll have the chance to push beyond your limits. You may also have other traits or characteristics that you'll have to overcome or modify in order to be most effective in your parenting.

I found this out early on. As a person prone to impatience, I had to learn to push beyond my limits to become a more patient parent to Jessica. If I had continued to express my impatience every time I felt it, I would have destroyed Jessica's fledgling sense of self-esteem and self-confidence. Because it takes her a long time to learn things, I have had to learn to appreciate the effort that she puts into the process, rather than focusing on how long it takes her to master a skill. At first being patient was like pulling thorns from my skin. Really, really hard, even painful.

But drawing on my experience in martial arts, I realized that learning to be patient was just like pushing beyond my limits in the *dojo* (training hall). When I thought I could do only ten kicks, the instructors encouraged me to do twenty. When I tested for rank promotion, I thought I'd never make it through the test—but I pushed hard and did it. I realized that in the same way, I could learn to acknowledge my impatience—just as in training I might acknowledge my fatigue—and push beyond it. Acknowledge it, but not act on it.

When I have the occasional impulse to be impatient now, I can recognize it. Immediately, I take a deep breath and consciously choose to push beyond that limit. I find that I am more relaxed and patient in all circumstances—in my work, with my friends and colleagues. It's a more enjoyable way to live but I would never have found this more pleasant way to be if I hadn't been determined to push beyond my limits as a mother.

Exercise

Identify the one limit you have that may be holding you back as a parent. It could be a personality trait, like my impatience. It could be an expectation or preconceived notion you have, such as "good" mothers never get frustrated. It could be something material, like not having a lot of money. One of the ways to identify what's holding you back is to create an "I wish" list, in relation to your child or children. On the list, write down the things you feel unhappy or guilty about doing or not doing, things you wish you had or could do or wish you didn't have or didn't do. The idea isn't to beat yourself up over all sorts of imagined wrongs, but to gain some clarity about what might be limiting you.

For example, my wish list might say something like: I wish Jessica would learn things faster, I wish I didn't get stressed when she repeats the same question five times. To me, that indicates that impatience is something I struggle with and that I should direct some of my energy to developing patience and learning to take a deep breath and count to ten.

Or, another example: After I got divorced and Jessica and the dogs and I moved into a rental duplex, my wish list then would have said: I wish I had a house. I wish Jessica and the dogs had a backyard to run around in. I wish I could decorate her room the way she wants. As you can see, these wishes relate to the concern about not having enough money to buy a house. But when I really looked at my wish list, I realized that although it would be nice for us to have a house, what is more important is for me to put my energy into being a loving and attentive parent. We could probably have the house sooner if I were willing to put in eighty hours of work a week, but that contradicts one of my cherished priorities, which is to spend all the time I can with Jessica. By letting go of that expectation—that everyone must have a house—and by thinking about the good life Jessica and I can have anyway, I don't spend a lot of unnecessary time and energy worrying about whether the roof over our head is rented or mortgaged. And that makes my life happier and more satisfying.

You, too, can push beyond any or all of these limits if you're creative and believe in yourself.

8

Learn with your child

As a mother, all knowledge, even that which seems useless (I'm thinking here of the baseball stats my brother used to memorize by the thousands), can help your own child learn to love learning. By respecting knowledge, you're teaching your child a valuable lesson. Go ahead and be impressed when someone (your kindergartener?) tells you all about how volcanoes are formed even though you'll never use those facts to further your career or improve your mothering skills.

Often, we think of knowledge as a commodity that will help us in our lives or our careers. We learn how to cook so that we can feed ourselves. We read trade magazines so that we stay abreast of what's happening in our industry. We read parenting magazines to get ideas for handling discipline problems. However, it's easy to get overloaded with all the information that lands on our doorsteps every day and to discount and devalue it. But it's important not to confuse information with knowledge. I agree that it's easy to have too much information. I'm not so sure anyone can have too much knowledge.

When I began training in the martial arts, I was shown what a front kick looks like. That was information. When I acquired the skill to do the front kick myself, that was knowledge. Like all martial artists, I was given opportunities to gain knowledge of many obscure techniques. For instance, the staff block, which I perfected as a brown belt. If someone comes charging after me with a staff, I'll know exactly what to do. Of course, it's much more likely that someone will come charging after me with a fist or a baseball bat or maybe even a knife, and in that case, knowing how to do the staff block isn't going to help me much. But that's not the point. The point is that the training has imparted knowledge far beyond the mere performance of a staff block. It has given me the knowledge that I can take on a challenge (like a disturbed individual with a baseball bat) and escape without too much damage to me or said individual. But if I had dismissed the knowledge—no one uses staffs to attack!—I would have missed some important learning.

Because children are so curious, you can feed and encourage their curiosity by learning more yourself. When Jessica started asking me about the moon and the stars, I realized how little I knew about them. Although I won't ever need to know for my own purposes (my opportunities for becoming an astronaut or an astronomer have long since passed), I found out as much as I could about the moon and the planets to share with her. Even if I weren't homeschooling her, this would be something I would do (at least I hope I'd do it!) The surprising thing is that this knowledge enriches my own life, even though I went years and years without knowing it. It's fun to share Jessica's excitement of discovery as we spot the moon every evening and see it wax and wane over the month. It makes me feel connected to the universe. And I can impress my friends by knowledgeably pointing out, "Full moon tomorrow; according to astrologers, that means good fortune!"

Exercise

Become involved in learning with your children. Not only is this likely to inspire them to learn, it creates opportunities for you to parent, to teach and to guide your child. When your toddler first says the word "dog!" don't just be pleased that she's learning to speak. Find a picture book about dogs in the library. Point out that dogs have ears, like people, and noses like people, that they have paws instead of hands and feet, that they have tails, which people don't, that they bark instead of using words. Get crayons and paper and help your little one draw pictures of the dogs in the neighborhood. Explain some basic rules for behaving with dogs: treating them gently, asking permission before touching an unknown dog, leaving the dog alone if it growls or barks. While your two-year-old may not understand everything you're saying, you're creating a solid foundation for the future.

When your five-year-old expresses an interest in rocks, don't simply nod and smile and go back to reading the newspaper. Go to the library with your child, look up books on rocks and minerals, visit a natural history museum, collect rocks outside. Your child may never become a geologist, but you'll inspire a love of learning and show your child how to discover knowledge on his own.

9
Mothering requires perseverance

No one gets the jump spinning wheel kick right on the first try. Only through repeated effort—perseverance—did I ever learn the technique. It took me years of working at it, but eventually the practice paid off.

I was able to apply this lesson to other parts of my life. When I had difficulties in graduate school, or problems establishing myself as a writer, I persevered. But never more than when I became a mother. Who knew that teaching a child to use the toilet would require every ounce of energy and ingenuity I possessed?

It can take a lot of perseverance to become the mother you want to be, to teach your child what you think is important, to provide moral and ethical guidance. If you have a colicky baby, and you think that one more night of walking the floor trying to soothe a screaming infant will truly send you round the bend, you're probably smart enough to seek advice (which I would encourage you to do despite what I am about to say next). According to my research, here's a summary of all the latest, most-advanced medical advice about colic (which about 20 percent of infants have): 1. Some babies feel better if their diet is changed (if feeding a formula, switch brands; if breast-feeding, modify your own diet). 2. It's okay for you to feel frustrated. 3. Take a deep breath. 4. Pat the baby's tummy. 5. Carry the baby around. That's it. That's the culmination of centuries' worth of medical information for an extremely common condition. Fat lot of help that is, right?

In other words, in the absence of more helpful information, all you can do is repeat Dory's mantra from *Finding Nemo* (and if you haven't seen this little gem yet, I assure you, you will). Dory says, "Just keep swimmin', swimmin'. What do we do? We swim, swim, swim." One of my friends claims that some days those are the only words that come out of her mouth.

When trying to solve a problem such as finding a discipline method that works for you and your child, you can easily be reduced to tears of frustration. The parenting books make it sound so easy—"put the child in time out, one minute per year of age." As so many mothers have told me, "Yeah, right." Sometimes the advice is "Ignore the misbehavior because it's simply done to get attention." As one mother commented to me, "My six-year-old pulls the phone right out of my hands. That's a little hard to ignore." Since one-size solutions don't fit all families and all circumstances, you need to have perseverance to find the right answers for you and your child. And of course what these right answers are will change over time.

As Emily Post once commented, "Any child can be taught to be beautifully behaved with no greater effort than quiet patience and perseverance." Of course, Emily also said, "Training a child is exactly like training a puppy."

One of the greatest rewards of using perseverance in your mothering is that it's a behavior—a habit—that you can pass along to your children. If your children see you persisting, trying again, keeping at it, they'll be more likely to do so for themselves. And if you encourage them and offer support as they try to master and accomplish the skills and tasks that are essential to childhood, they will appreciate that the struggle has its rewards. Then when faced with challenges throughout their lives, they will be well equipped to handle them. The most important thing to remember when trying to teach persistence and perseverance is not to do their job yourself. This is easier said than done—we want to help our children and give them the best. But imagine how struggling and achieving can help build a child's self-confidence. I know a mother whose daughter was born without arms. When she felt her daughter was capable of doing so, one day she placed an outfit on the bed, told her daughter to come downstairs for breakfast when she was dressed and left the room. Imagine how difficult that was for the mother! But she knew it had to be done if she had any hope of her daughter ever becoming an independent adult. I'm sure there were tears of rage and frustration on everyone's part . . . but eventually the daughter came down for breakfast, fully dressed. Knowing that she could do it. Can you think of anything more powerful for a child than that?

E x e r c i s e

Commit to persevering when you're teaching your child something important. Don't give up too soon or think your child is too young to learn. It may be unfair to discipline your child for not saying "Thanks" when she's eighteen months old, but it's not too early to prompt your child— "Say, 'Thank you'"—and then reward any effort to comply. Keep encouraging the behavior you want and eventually your child will display it without your prompting. It may take longer than you'd believe possible, but the effort will bring rewards.

In the same way, encourage persistence in your children. Believe it or not, games like peek-a-boo and make-believe actually help young children develop longer attention spans and encourage persistence. If your child loves playing a certain game over and over, go ahead and play it with her five times. If she has trouble pulling her pants up after going potty, don't immediately rush to her aid— let her do it herself. Tell her "You can do it!" and give her a big, encouraging grin. Some children have more self-doubt than others and may need to be encouraged to do more things independently. Show them that *you* have no doubt in them at all.

10

Flexible mothers are strong ones

Martial artists know that "power" is more than just mass directed at a target. Speed and flexibility also measure into the equation. (I mean this literally: The physics equation for force is mass times velocity equals force. Martial artists think of this as mass times speed equals power.) To have speed, you must be flexible, and too much mass prevents you from being flexible. In other words, if you're big but you can't kick above the ankle, you're at a disadvantage to someone who can. So martial artists value flexibility and realize it brings them strength. They train to be more flexible and work on it just as much—perhaps more—than on pure muscle (mass) building.

It's good to remember that in the same way, a flexible parent can be strong. We all know people who are inflexible and unbending and we wouldn't necessarily call them joyful, loving parents. Adhering to a rigid set of rules doesn't necessarily produce the desired effect, which is happy, productive adults (or at least something along those lines). Certainly there are issues on which you should not bend. But there are many times when being flexible makes you stronger as a parent.

This means letting your child make choices—including choices you wouldn't necessarily make. Letting your four-year-old choose her clothes, even if her outfit isn't what you'd pick, teaches her to rely on herself to get dressed. It doesn't matter if the shirt is yellow paisley, the pants are blue plaid and the shoes are red with rhinestones. It looks lovely because your child did it herself.

Suzan Erem, who co-authored the book *Do I Want to Be a Mom? A Woman's Guide to the Decision of a Lifetime,* interviewed dozens of mothers for her book. She says, "The main advice was 'be flexible.' If women were control freaks, it didn't go well with the kids, or else they raised [children with all the confidence and motivation of] mushrooms. But if they could remain flexible—from the clutter on the floor caused by a two-year-old to the belly-piercing their teenager came home with, they were good." The parents and the children were happy, had better relationships with one another, and the children grew up to be more confident, happy adults. "It probably has something to do with respecting people for who they are, no matter their age," Suzan says.

Being able to respect your child and what she wants and needs is important to being flexible. My sister Beth, a quality assurance manager and the mother of a two-year-old, remembers one Sunday night when her daughter, Alexis, was having a hard time settling down and needed her mother to hold her. "I ended up holding her all night," Beth says. "I knew it seemed different somehow, and that it was important for me to be there, so I didn't insist that she go to her crib." The next morning, Alexis was still clinging tenaciously to her mother. "I called in to work and took a vacation day," Beth says. "It was very obvious that something was going on with Alexis and she just needed the reassurance that I was there and would always be there for her." By afternoon, Alexis was scampering around as usual, and her mother was able to go back to her normal routine. "I think if I had insisted that she sleep in her own bed that night, and if I had gone off to work like usual, she would have felt a strong sense of abandonment," says Beth. But by being flexible and letting go of the rules, Beth was able to reinforce her daughter's trust. Now Alexis has no problems when Beth heads off for work in the morning, securely knowing that her mother will be home in time for dinner.

Of course it's always important to enforce the rules when a child's safety and well-being are at stake—it's never okay to run into the street or stick forks in the electrical outlet—but for matters of lesser importance, being flexible can make you a stronger mother, and can reinforce your bonds with your children.

Exercise

Consider the rules and expectations you have for your children. Are there times when you could be more flexible? Could you be as effective—or possibly more effective—if you relaxed things a bit? If your infant finds a pacifier soothing, why not let her have one (at least until she's a bit older)? If your toddler feels strongly about bringing his lovey (usually a stained and decrepit stuffed bear) everywhere, including church, the park, the grocery store and the bathroom, why not let him? If your kindergartener doesn't fold the laundry the way you do, at least the laundry is getting folded. If your grade-schooler wants to learn ballet and you think soccer is a better sport, does it really matter? At least your child is getting an activity in. Why not choose to be flexible when you can?

II

A wise mother masters many techniques

A wise woman knows that she can't face every challenge in the same way. A demoralizing boss and an ill friend each require a different spirit, approach and demeanor. The wise woman taps her creativity and uses different techniques to solve different problems.

Mastering many parenting techniques reduces conflict and contributes to being an effective mother. It's especially important if you have more than one child, because you relate to each child in a different way. They need you to respond to them individually, according to your own unique relationship. In my own childhood, my five siblings and I were all quite different temperamentally. If my parents simply threatened to be disappointed in me, that was enough to make me comply with their rules and expectations. But one of my sisters wasn't bothered if my parents were disappointed in her. She thought it was too bad, but it wasn't persuasive enough to make her change her behavior. When disciplining her, my parents had to try a different strategy. She responded better to concrete consequences such as taking away privileges.

A wise warrior knows she will be defeated in battle if all she can do is one technique. If she can do a front kick and that's it, her opponent will easily be able to block the kick and counterattack. She will be helpless to prevent it. In the same way, if you rely on only one technique to deal with your children's problems, it will soon become ineffective. If all you can do when a child misbehaves is yell at him, pretty soon the child will stop listening to your yelling and it won't achieve the results you're hoping for.

The warrior learns many different techniques for those occasions when the front kick isn't enough. Having a variety of techniques—kicks and punches and throws and blocks and deflections—means she is more likely to be successful if she's forced to defend herself.

In other words, when you're trying to quiet a crying baby and singing lullabies doesn't help, try taking a walk around the living room, blowing bubbles in the backyard, going for a ride in the car, giving a gentle tummy or back massage. And if all else fails, call your best friend and ask her to come over and let you take a break.

And although a warrior doesn't use all the techniques in every single match, she does train in them. They're there if she needs them. Having them in her arsenal makes her more confident. Her confidence actually helps prevent problems from even happening. So a wise mother knows to keep other parenting strategies in mind for when she needs them.

Exercise

Think up new strategies for dealing with the same old problems instead of repeating the same old techniques that get you nowhere. And realize that as children grow, what used to work may no longer do so. Once Jessica was three, my singing a song to her no longer had the power to soothe her when she was upset. But I was able to teach her how to take a deep breath and get control over her own emotions. That was a powerful skill for her to learn. She still uses it regularly when she feels upset and wants to calm down so she can communicate with me.

Some children will actually want to be involved in this process of figuring out strategies, so include them. One child I know functions best when she and her parents sit down and go over their expectations for her behavior, clearly laying out what will happen if she breaks a rule. She prefers to have it written down in detail. For other children, this would be overkill and they'd feel their lives were being run in too rigid and regimented a way. So keep your child's temperament in mind as you explore new ways of handling your relationships with your kids.

Be creative. It's easy to fall back on the yell-at-'em routine, but by mastering many techniques you can be more effective and can reduce the conflict in your relationships with your children.

12

Discipline brings power to you and your child

Discipline is not the same thing as punishment, so forget that connection for a moment. The two are related, of course, both in martial arts and in parenting. But discipline, by itself, is simply the art of doing what needs to be done—doing what you say you're going to do. And that's a powerful and freeing thing, for both you and your child. It creates a sense of safety, stability and predictability, values that are important in family life.

We sometimes use the words "punishment" and "discipline" as if they were the same thing, and it's important to remember that they're not. In martial arts, discipline means that you get to your feet and bow to the instructor when she enters the room, no matter what else you happen to be doing at the time. Punishment is the fifty push-ups you have to do if you fail to do so.

Putting this in a parenting context, discipline is making your bed every morning, and punishment is not being able to watch your favorite television show when you fail to make your bed. It's important to make these consequences clear—that's part of discipline. It's also important to remember that encouragement can be much more powerful than punishment, and that you can use encouragement to produce discipline (see Lesson #20).

For children, discipline is important because it gives structure to their days. They know that they'll get up at a certain time and eat breakfast first thing and that they're then responsible for getting dressed for school. They know where the school bus stop is and they know when to expect lunch and they know what to do when they come home from school and you're still at work, because you've already explained the rules.

This doesn't mean that you can't sometimes be flexible (see Lesson #10). It just means that it's important to be flexible within a framework of discipline. For example, you can be flexible about what your child chooses to wear to school but you can be disciplined about expecting your child to be ready when the school bus arrives at 7:15 a.m.

Consistently applying the rules is the cornerstone of successful discipline. If it's sometimes okay to leave your toys scattered around the living room and sometimes it's not, the child receives a confusing and contradictory message and is more likely to ignore your demands that he clean up his toys because he knows from experience that it's not an expectation you always have.

Instilling discipline in your children doesn't have to be painful or difficult, if you're creative. When my sister Beth is in a parking lot or crowded store with her two-year-old, Alexis, the rule is that Alexis must hold her hand. This is an important safety issue. If Alexis balks, then Beth picks her up and carries her or puts her in a shopping cart. Alexis would much rather walk than be carried or pushed in a cart or stroller, so this "punishment" teaches her the consequences of refusing to follow the rules. Simple, but effective.

Other appropriate responses to inappropriate behavior might be to leave the store without buying the stickers your child wanted or to cut the play date short if she won't share. You can also weather a rough patch by removing the stimulus to inappropriate behavior—for instance, restricting television viewing if your children are starting to behave like the cartoon characters they love, calling for delivery rather than trying to dine at a restaurant when your toddler is at the stage where she just can't sit still or confiscating all the balls if your children can't seem to keep from throwing them at each other indoors.

For older children, you can be open about the importance of discipline. Talk with your child about how it takes discipline to go to work every day, but that the reward is you earn money for food and rent and trips to the zoo. Point out that their going to school every day is the same kind of discipline, and praise them for it. Do things together to get into the habit of having discipline. Fold the laundry together, clean the house together, run errands together. Show how having discipline contributes to the family good, and so it's more than just doing something for yourself. Children like to know that their actions are meaningful to others and feel powerful and important when they contribute to their family life.

Exercise

For very young children, keeping to schedules is the beginning of discipline. Try to be consistent about bedtimes, naptimes and mealtimes, and that will help your child get into a comforting, reliable routine (which is basically what discipline is—acting in a consistent way all the time, and doing what you say you're going to do). Turning actions into habits means there's less struggle and conflict in your relationships with your children. The more you can make actions into scheduled habits, the easier it is to instill discipline in your children. For instance, if the action you want is for your child to make his bed, to turn it into a habit, help him make his bed before he does anything else in the morning. Soon (okay, maybe not so soon), making the bed will become a simple matter of routine and your child won't think anything about it.

Having discipline yourself makes it easier to encourage it in your child. So if you set the example of eating right and doing your chores in a timely fashion, it's more likely that your child will follow along—or at the least, your struggles to encourage discipline in your child won't feel hypocritical.

If you feel that you're not as disciplined as you could be in some aspects of your life—for example, saving for college or retirement, getting enough exercise—make a commitment to working on being more disciplined in these areas, not just for your own sake but for your children, too. Show them what you're doing to be disciplined and help them understand why it's an important skill to develop.

13

Integrity in all actions creates confidence

Every now and then, I'll read about some disgraced CEO who's going to prison for lying, cheating or stealing or some combination thereof, and I wonder how his children must feel. If there's one thing I could always count on in my life, it was that my parents would never go to prison for lying, cheating or stealing. They had unshakeable integrity. I had friends who didn't feel this way about their parents. It could have been their mother or father up there and it wouldn't have surprised them a whole lot. I remember how sorry I always felt for them. What a cloud for a child to live under.

As a parent, I have always placed a high priority on having integrity in all my actions—not just those that directly affect my child—because I want Jessica to grow up with the same sure knowledge I had. And the truth is, if you have integrity in only certain parts of your life, you don't really have integrity at all.

In the martial arts, integrity is one of the characteristics you're expected to develop in your training. The idea isn't that you'll be rewarded for having integrity—sometimes having integrity is exactly what gets you fired from your job. The idea is that having integrity makes you a stronger, more confident, more trustworthy individual. People can count on you if you have integrity. And integrity isn't what happens when other people are watching you. Integrity is what happens when no one is looking. In the martial arts, we practice integrity when we work as hard when we're training solo as we do when we're being judged by the promotion committee. We show integrity by honoring the martial arts and never misusing them.

When you have integrity in your life, you don't always take the easy road, the path of least resistance. You do what you know is right. If you have a moral conviction, then you defend it. Your children can see the importance of integrity in life if you show it in all of your actions and in all of your dealings.

That's why it's important to mention it when the cashier mistakenly gives you change for $20 when you handed her a $10 bill. Maybe the clerk was so rude you feel she "owes" it to you. But your children are watching. If for no other reason, that ought to convince you to correct the error. In the same way, when the annoying next door neighbor calls, don't say to your husband, "Tell her I'm not here." Your kid sees you sitting right there, and deduces that in fact sometimes it *is* okay to lie. If you're supposed to pay train fare for your child, you don't tell him to duck under the turnstile to save yourself a couple of bucks. Your child will see how you act honestly and with integrity in the little things as well as in the big things. It makes you a good role model for your child, and it gives your child faith and trust in you—you're reliable, you mean what you say and you do what you say.

Exercise

Take the opportunity to show integrity in your life, even in small things that you normally don't think twice about. Instead of using the copier at work to make fifty copies of your son's resume, send your son to the local copy center. You'll be sending an important message at the same time.

At the same time, be sure you stress the importance of integrity in your child's own actions. Children begin learning right from wrong at a very young age. If your toddler grabs a candy bar off the rack at the grocery store and you don't notice it until you're out in the parking lot, don't just shrug it off by thinking you spend enough money there to cover the loss. Bring your toddler inside, return the candy bar, apologize to the clerk or manager and explain to your child why what he did was wrong: "We can't just take, we have to pay for things." "You have to ask Mama's permission first."

Creating an environment where integrity is prized means that your children know they can rely on you. They know that you will support them when they do the right thing. They know that you will be there to help them understand what the right thing is. When they come home from school with an ethical dilemma, they know they can talk it over with you. They don't have to find out from someone else if it's okay to tattle on a friend if he's in danger of doing someone harm. You can tell them what you believe, and why you believe it and guide them as they make their own choices.

14

Know what results you want for your child

As mothers, most of us want many of the same things for our children. We want them to be happy and healthy. We want them to have a satisfying purpose in their life, whether that's raising their own kids, or volunteering at the humane society, or pursuing their passion for the Dewey decimal system by becoming a librarian. We want them to have enjoyable lives and to get along with their loved ones.

If we start with those ends in mind, we can shape our actions to encourage our children to grow up healthy and happy, to find a purpose and learn how to get along with other people.

It's when we start to think about what we want *from* our children that we run into trouble. We want them to love us forever with the same unreserved heart-stopping love we have for them. We want them to stay close to us. We want them to give us grandchildren. We want them to do us proud and support us in our old age. And when we want our children to fulfill dreams and fantasies we had for ourselves, we also run into trouble—when we decide we never want them to be frustrated a day in their lives, we want them to avoid all of the mistakes we've made and we want them to have everything we never did and be everything we never were. That's when we've moved from good, solid parenting to something a little more selfish, a little more about us than about our children.

A martial artist knows that even before she starts working with a partner, sparring an opponent, or defending herself against an attacker, she must first figure out what she wants to get out of it. If she's working with a partner, maybe she wants to improve her timing, or her speed, or her technique. If she decides she wants to impress the onlookers with how cute she looks in her uniform, she's probably got the wrong goal in mind. Impressing the onlookers won't make her a better martial artist. If she's sparring an opponent, she has to know what she wants—which may be to win the match, to demonstrate some difficult techniques or simply to put up a good fight against a superior opponent. If her goal is to win at any cost, even if it requires hitting illegal target areas or using too much force, again, she's probably got the wrong goal. If she's defending herself against an attacker, again, she has to decide what she wants: Is it to get away, to draw attention to the attack, to disarm the attacker, to disable him? If her goal is not to embarrass herself, she's probably got the wrong goal. Once she decides what she wants to get out of the situation, she chooses techniques and strategies that will get her what she wants. She will use different techniques if she's just trying to get away from the attacker and run back into the mall than if she's trying to disable the attacker and render him harmless.

In just the same way, if you choose what you want for

your child, you can choose the techniques that will likely get you there. Create a philosophy of the results you want for your child. It should go something like, *I want my child to be a productive member of society,* or *I want my child to pursue her passion,* or *I want my child to value her relationships.* Then you can create a series of steps and strategies to achieve those results. If you don't know what you want for your child, then you'll have a hard time taking the right steps to provide what she needs.

Exercise

Sit down with those who are important in your child's life (father, grandparents, stepfather) and talk about what you want for your child. What results do you want? How can you help your child get there? If your child is old enough to be involved in the conversation, invite him. It's important for him to see that you care about how what happens now will affect his future. For example, suppose you decide that the main result you want is for your child to be a productive member of society, and to ensure this, you feel he must have a good education.

Determine what actions you will take. When your child is little, perhaps you stimulate his brain and his imagination by playing classical music in the background, inviting him to explore the world, restricting television and video watching. As he gets older, you choose a Montessori preschool that helps him learn at his own pace and discover what he likes to do. Or perhaps instead you choose a more traditionally focused academic classroom to better prepare him for the rigors of a classical education.

As your child reaches grade school age, you have more choices to make. If your public school system is unsatisfactory, will you need to move? Or make sacrifices to send your child to private school?

Will you homeschool your child? Hire a tutor? Your choices don't have to be expensive or time-consuming or even popular with the neighbors. They just need to help you achieve the result you want.

15

Teach others and you will learn

When I began training in the martial arts, I was surprised to learn that I was expected to "teach" from the moment I stepped onto the mat. When I worked with another student, I was supposed to help him learn the techniques and memorize the forms. Later, I was expected to assist the instructor at classes, going around the room and showing people how to do the techniques correctly. I was expected to lead classes now and then, to step in when the instructor was sick or called away. Finally, I became a teacher.

At each stage of the process, I learned more than I taught. I had to know the techniques extremely well in order to show them and describe them to other students. I had to understand their purpose, and I had to understand why we did them the way we did them. And when my students started learning more difficult techniques, I had to push myself to stay a step ahead of them.

New parents might be surprised to learn that they, too, have a great deal to teach even if they are beginners. Often they feel overwhelmed by the experience of caring for a newborn, and they seek advice and help, and that's good. But they often also downplay their own ability to teach—and I don't just mean the teaching that you do for your child. I mean the teaching that you do for other parents and other children. The more you teach, the more you learn. The more you're out there trying to show what a good parent does, the more you become a good parent.

Your teaching can take many forms. It might be joining a group of new mothers, or a support group for parents of special-needs children, or it might be simple conversations you have with friends. Don't be afraid to share what you've learned and don't feel that you have to have had seven children and thirty years of child-rearing to have something useful to contribute. But you have to be open to learning from your teaching.

Exercise

Find a way that you can contribute as a teacher, no matter where you are as a parent—veteran mother of adult children or brand-new mom. Maybe there's something you do, such as yoga, that you can teach mothers and their children. Maybe you can be part of a local "Parents as Teachers" group that helps less fortunate families raise their children well. Maybe you can volunteer to teach art at your children's school since budget cuts have eliminated this in many areas. Teach and you will learn.

16

Physical strength creates mental and emotional strength

Mothers must have mental and emotional stamina. They also need physical strength. The combination helps you get through the challenges of an ordinary—or even not so ordinary—day. Remember a time when you felt overwhelmed and out of balance, as if every problem you had had suddenly spiraled out of control? You probably felt tired, distracted and unfocused at the time. By staying physically fit, you'll help reduce the number of times when everything spirals out of control.

When martial artists train, they try to develop endurance and strength so that they can get through the physical challenges of competing in tournaments, doing well on promotion tests and mastering the techniques of the martial arts. Not surprisingly, they find that physical, mental and emotional strength are linked. If they're having an emotionally difficult day, they're less able to do the physical tasks of training. If they feel mentally distracted and unfocused, they have less success in their training. At the same time, the opposite, positive side is also true. When they feel emotionally and mentally prepared, they feel physically stronger. And when they've gained physical strength, they find they've gained more emotional and mental stamina as well.

Making physical strength (through physical exercise) a priority helps you maintain not just your health and fitness, but your stability and balance. It makes you a more effective parent. The task of juggling a shifting load of work, priorities and needs can be exhausting, and having reserves of strength—physical, mental and emotional—is necessary. It's also important to know those reserves are available. To know they're available, you have to train, you have to draw on those resources. Having done so makes you more confident that you can get through today's challenges and crises just as you managed yesterday's.

Exercise

If you don't have a program for staying physically strong, get one. Make it a priority. It doesn't have to be something that eats up precious hours every day, and it doesn't have to be something expensive, difficult to do or distasteful. Bring your kids to the park and jog around the play area while they climb around on the slides. Put up a basketball hoop in the driveway and challenge your teenager to a duel every evening after work. Take a mother-and-baby yoga class at the local parks and recreation program.

If you already have a program for staying strong, commit to it and know that it makes you a stronger, more capable mother.

17

Understand what is expected of you as a mother

For a martial artist at the beginning stage of her training, what is expected of her is simple: She'll come to class regularly, apply herself to learning the techniques and listen courteously to the instructor. While these expectations don't require a degree in rocket science, many people have difficulty meeting them because they don't realize what's expected of them. They don't look around and observe and deduce that if they come to class regularly, try to learn and listen, they'll do fine. Sometimes they think it must be more complicated than that. Sometimes they're simply not paying attention.

For parents, it's important to understand what is expected of you—not in the sense of what the neighbor thinks you should do or what your mother's priorities are—but rather what you must do in order to do your job right. Miryam Williamson, who raised three children and one foster child single-handedly, says, "Motherhood is not a popularity contest. Don't campaign for them to love (or even like) you. Teach them what they must know to live comfortably in the world. When they grow up, they'll thank you for it. . . . Actually several of my kids *have* thanked me." And that's a very good starting point: What's expected of you is to socialize and civilize your children so that they can go out in public and not destroy the fabric of civilization.

As a mother, understanding what was expected of me was pretty simple and straightforward at first. Because Jessica was born with a placid, friendly nature, I felt from the very beginning that what was expected of me as a mother was this: Don't screw her up. She already seems to have the innate ability to be happy and to flourish, so I just need to encourage that and do my best not to quash it. And this was quite simple when she was young. I just gave her lots of love and attention and she was fine. But as she grows older, the process becomes more difficult. I have to also teach her important skills like getting along with other people, focusing on a task until it's done, learning to read. And if I'm not careful, I could squash her sweet nature by demanding strict obedience and acting like a drill sergeant. But if I don't have some rules in place for her, and if I don't enforce discipline when necessary, she won't learn important things like getting along with other people and how to read books.

Sometimes what's expected of us is to be able to deal with the conflicts fulfilling our role creates. As psychiatrist Elaine Heffner points out, "[It's] important for a mother to know that the process of growing up involves by definition things that her child is not going to like. Her job is not to create a bed of roses but to help him learn how to pick his way through the thorns."

By understanding what is expected of you as a parent, you can put your energies toward creating a relationship with your children that results in their being loved, fed, clothed, sheltered, educated and respecting of themselves and others. Chances are this will, in the end, make them happy. But you can't be happy for them or make them happy. That's their responsibility—that's what's expected of *them*.

What you need to do to be an effective parent changes over time. When your children are young, you'll need to do certain things (feed them and change them and protect them) and as they grow older, you'll need to do certain things that are sometimes the opposite of what you did when they were younger (expect them to feed themselves and change themselves and send them off into the cold cruel world without you hovering near).

Take stock of where you are right now. What are the expectations for this stage of your child's life? Should you be letting go, or expecting more? Should you be supervising more or less? Remember that just as the expectations of the martial artist change as she moves through the ranks, so will the expectations of the parent change as the child matures.

18
Courtesy reveals your strength

Some people think courtesy—which they equate with "manners"—is optional, unnecessary, hopelessly plebian. But consider: Who is more impressive, the person who is gracious in all circumstances, or the person who screams obscenities every time some little thing goes wrong? Who do we think is calmer, stronger? The one making hand gestures, or the one who shrugs off the behavior of a rude salesclerk? At dinner with friends, who is most likely to have pleasant encounters with others and to find her life more enjoyable, the one yakking on the cell phone, oblivious to the friends who are waiting to have dinner with her? Or the one who arrives on time, gives her full attention to her friends and doesn't make anyone uncomfortable by insulting the waiter for not being quick enough with the water glasses?

Courtesy—making an effort to be considerate to others— reveals your strength. But in our casual society, formal courtesy is rare outside the *dojo* (training hall). In the *dojo,* traditional martial artists perform traditional courtesies. They bow when they enter the *dojo*; they bow to senior students and the instructor; they don't interrupt a senior student or instructor when she is doing something else; they use titles such as "*sensei*" and "*sabumnim*" and "sir" and "ma'am." This helps them show respect for the art and for each other.

My martial arts training helped me see that using courtesy in the world outside the *dojo* resulted in a more pleasant existence in the world. The clerks at the post office started calling me by name. The tellers at the bank traded jokes with me. When a driver cut me off in traffic, I ignored it. I didn't get enraged or feel tense or trade insults for insults. I felt stronger and more confident. It wasn't about me. It was about someone else being a jerk. Occasionally I would set boundaries because treating me disrespectfully is not acceptable, but for the most part, if I was courteous to other people, they were courteous to me.

Miryam Williamson points out that teaching courtesy serves another purpose: "My kids thank me now because they feel at ease in situations that make most people feel awkward."

I have to admit that even though I knew this—I knew courtesy was important, I had seen it in my martial arts experience and in my own life—when Jessica was born, I tended to let her get away with antisocial behavior because, well, gee, she had all these problems and I hated to be mean to her by expecting high standards of behavior . . . she couldn't help it that she was different, right?

Then I had an educational experience: One day I was in the waiting room at a neurologist's office, and a woman walked in with a child about two years old who had obvious facial deformities. My first feeling was one of compassion. But when he started screaming at his mother, shoving the other children aside, grabbing their toys and otherwise being extremely rude and unpleasant, while his mother made no move to correct his behavior, I took a strong dislike to him (and to her). I realized that she wasn't doing him any favors by letting him act like that. His life was going to be difficult enough, given his differences. She didn't need to compound the problem by letting him turn into a holy terror that no child (or adult) would want to be around.

From that moment on, I taught Jessica to be courteous. I insisted that she learn to say "please" and "thank you." Now she waves at clerks and says, "Thank you! See you next time!" Sometimes she'll say, "Thank you for coming!" when in fact we were the ones who came, but I'm sure she'll figure that out eventually. She never fails to elicit a grin on even the most glum, humbug face. People remark on how pleasant she is and say that she is a very generous and kind person. I think this is important. I want people to be able to get to know Jessica and realize that she is charming and a lot of fun to be around. I don't want her manners or her attitude to put people off. I realized she would get a lot further in life if people found it pleasant to be around her, and this was one thing I could teach her.

For her, being courteous is rewarded. People smile and

give her hugs when she is. She feels valued and respected—something I have always been concerned that she might not feel. In other words, she teaches other people how to treat her. By being courteous she teaches them to treat her courteously.

Exercise

Model courtesy for your children. If you're constantly screaming at salesclerks and giving in to road rage, your children will probably follow suit. By holding your temper and being pleasant and courteous, you show your children how to do the same.

You should be courteous to your children and your loved ones just as you are to strangers. When your child folds the laundry, you should say "Thank you," even if that's his job, because you should appreciate it when people do helpful tasks. When you cook a meal, your children should say, "Thank you," even if they don't like green beans, because you went to the trouble of making the meal for them and they should acknowledge that.

Courtesy really does begin at home. There's absolutely nothing wrong—and everything right—with telling your children "Please" and "I'm glad you did that" and "Excuse me." Getting into the habit of courtesy makes everyone feel valued and appreciated, and by being courteous we teach others to be courteous to us.

19
The wise mother does not reflect on past deeds

A martial artist works with partners who are more skilled than she is and partners who are less skilled. As she gets more skilled herself, she may do better against opponents who had previously been difficult for her to defeat. So even if her opponent won the match last time, it doesn't mean she'll win the match this time, too. If she underestimates the less-skilled opponent because she defeated her in the last match, the less-skilled opponent might defeat her in this match. She learns that the past doesn't predict the present. She concentrates on doing her best right now, in this match.

It's equally important for mothers to recognize that what has happened in the past doesn't necessarily determine what will happen now or in the future. Suppose, for example, that you're trying to help your child with her math homework, yet every time you do, the two of you get into a fight. The answer isn't to never help your child with math homework. The answer is to consider what you could do differently that might change the outcome, and then focus on this, rather than thinking about all the times your efforts to help have ended in a fight.

You might try a different strategy, such as having her older sister or her father help with the math homework. Or you might hire a math tutor. Or you might talk with her teacher about different ways to help with homework. You might bone up on math yourself and think up different approaches to helping her understand the concepts. Or you can simply decide that you won't get irritated when she howls for the tenth time, "I don't get it!" By concentrating on what you can do in the present and not focusing on the past, you'll be more likely to find a solution to your current difficulty. But if you keep telling yourself, "Whenever I try to help Jane with her math homework, we argue, so there's no use helping," you're focusing on the negative—you're focusing on past deeds. By moving beyond that focus, you can do what needs to be done to help Jane succeed at math class.

If your toddler "always" has a tantrum when you try to go out to eat with friends, that doesn't mean that your only choices are never eating out or hiring baby-sitters. Doing so means you're reflecting on past deeds. Instead, try new strategies. Try eating earlier or later or at a family-friendly restaurant. Start small—a ten-minute visit at the coffee shop. Reward good behavior and extend the interval.

Exercise

Banish "always" and "never" from your vocabulary, as in, "I always lose my temper when Joe doesn't clean his room" and "Joe never cleans his room." Those words indicate that you're focusing on the past. You need to remember that the present is all that matters, and that you can change your thoughts and your actions, and that these changes can result in the success you want.

20
Encouragement teaches more than punishment

When teaching rules to a child, you can choose to punish or you can choose to encourage (or you can choose some combination of punishment and encouragement). You can encourage him to obey or you can punish him for disobeying or you can encourage him to obey *and* punish him for disobeying.

In a martial arts school, it's a pretty common sight to see a kid who didn't listen in class doing ten push-ups as a way to reinforce the importance of good listening skills. It's a traditional "punishment." Punishments can work: "If you don't clean your room, you can't play with your friend Sarah this afternoon"; "If you miss the school bus, you'll be late and get a detention"; "If you talk back to your mother, no PlayStation for you this afternoon." You can describe what will happen to the child if he doesn't do as you say, and since most people dislike pain, he'll try to follow the rules in order to avoid it.

But punishments are by their nature negative. Even if you avoid the punishment, it's disheartening and dispiriting to have to listen to threats all the time. Very young children don't even understand punishment—they don't connect their actions to their punishment. So it's just bewildering and confusing to them if you punish them for misbehaving. If you threaten a nine-month-old with, "If you don't stop yelling at me, I'm not going to let you play with your blocks," you're not going to stop the yelling. For preschoolers, it can wear them down to hear what they feel is constant criticism: "Get off that chair or you're going to get into trouble," "Don't touch that or you're going to your room," "Stop pulling the cat's tail or no dessert for you!" After all, they're just doing what preschoolers do—exploring the world. For an older child, it's hard to feel great about saying, "Hey, I passed my math test and avoided getting grounded for two weeks!" Much better to tell your friends, "I passed my math test so my mom says I can have friends over for a get-together tonight."

No one likes to focus on the negative. Often, it's more effective to be positive—you're more likely to get the results you want. In other words, use encouragement: "If you make it to the bus stop on time, I won't have to drive you to school and therefore I'll have time to pick up the movie you wanted me to rent for this weekend." Sometimes, it's just a matter of changing how you phrase something: Instead of saying, "If you don't clean your room, you can't play with Sarah," you can say, "Once you clean your room, you can play with Sarah."

I first saw this principle in action when I began training in the martial arts. I sometimes broke a rule (usually inadvertently—I didn't realize the rule existed), which resulted in my having to do push-ups as punishment. The funny thing is, although I know I did some push-ups—I distinctly remember doing them—I have no idea what they were punishment for. I cannot remember what rule I broke. Which goes to show how much the punishment helped me remember the rules.

On the other hand, I can remember those times when the teacher made a special effort to encourage me: Once when we were doing a kicking drill and he said, "Your body line and position are perfect," I felt like I had won the lotto. Another time, an instructor asked me demonstrate my form in front of the class because I was doing it so well. I was a beginner at the time and there were black belts in the class, and this compliment made me feel I could do anything. But I'm telling you, I have no idea why I did the push-ups.

It's easy to fall into the routine of saying things like, "If you don't stop teasing the dogs, you're not going to watch *Finding Nemo* tonight before bed," especially if you're dealing with a little one who has ignored all of your previous attempts to get her to stop. But there are several problems with this "punishment" that can make it ineffective.

First, the punishment doesn't seem related to the teasing. What do teasing the dogs and watching *Finding Nemo* have to do with each other? If you're hoping to teach your child the consequences of her actions, the consequences should have something to do with the actions.

Second, the child can decide, as thousands have decided before her, that she doesn't want to watch *Finding Nemo* anyway. Which means that she won't stop teasing the dogs, and she won't be able to watch *Finding Nemo* and no one is satisfied.

Third, you're not giving her any tools to be successful— just a threat. And most of us resent threats. If your boss says, "Increase productivity by 20 percent this quarter," but doesn't give you the money, equipment or staff to do it, you're probably going to fail. Consider that your child has even fewer tools than you as an adult have, and even you sometimes need guidance to be more successful.

So how can you turn a punishment into an encouragement? One way is to turn it around. Think of watching *Find-*

ing Nemo as a reward. Would you say, "If you stop teasing the dogs, we'll be able to watch *Finding Nemo* now"? If yes, then why not phrase it that way? If not—you don't think it's right to bribe kids to do what you ask—then why would you give this kind of punishment? Because by saying, "No *Finding Nemo* if you don't stop teasing the dogs," you are in effect saying, "If you do stop teasing the dogs, you'll get to watch *Finding Nemo*."

Another way to turn a punishment into an encouragement is to decide what you want to teach about the problem behavior. When my niece Alexis discovered the joy of teasing her two dogs when she was not quite two, her mother, Beth, knew that she needed to find a way to teach Alexis not just that teasing the dogs was wrong, but why it was wrong. So she would say, "The dogs are living, breathing creatures, just like you, that we've promised to take care of. That means we have to love them and be gentle with them. Just as you wouldn't want them to tease you, they don't want you to tease them." But Alexis was only not quite two, and Beth knew the problem was going to require more than a short lecture to be resolved.

Then she struck on the idea of having Alexis participate in the dog care. Now, every morning she has the responsibility of feeding the dogs. She finds their bowls—she knows which dog gets which bowl—and scoops the dog food out of the big tub it's stored in, and alerts her parents when the water dishes are low. She helps her mother brush the dogs' coats several times a week. By learning to care for them in this way, she recognizes them as more than just large stuffed animals that move. She recognizes that they are animals that should be treated with love and gentleness. Isn't it much more encouraging to solve a problem this way—by focusing on how to actively involve your child in succeeding—instead of simply punishing misbehavior?

E x e r c i s e

Next time you think about punishing your child for a misdeed, think about how you can turn the punishment into an encouragement. Turn the negative into the positive and both you and your child will feel happier for it.

Children will remember the punishment—the push-ups—not the reason for them. But they will remember why and how you encouraged them, and that will go with them throughout their lives.

21

Practice patience as your child masters new skills

If I had known that learning to do a front kick would take 10,000 tries, I would probably have been a little less keen about signing up for martial arts lessons. Fortunately, no one told me this at first, and I just chugged along doing the best I could. By the time I realized how much effort goes into perfecting the front kick, I was hooked on martial arts, and I wasn't going to back out.

Mastery requires the willingness to do the same thing over and over. It requires us to give ourselves a break and to keep trying.

It's especially important to remember that mastery requires patience when it comes to our children. When they first learn to crawl and to walk and to read and to ride a bike, we have a tendency to think that it should be easier than it is. After all, look how easy it is for us to crawl and walk and read and ride bikes. But then, we have done the technique 10,000 times, so we know how to do it. Our children haven't done the technique 10,000 times.

Journalist Mary Kay Blakely writes about the patience required when children are learning new skills: "In the range of things toddlers have to learn and endlessly review—why you can't put bottles with certain labels in your mouth, why you can't take whatever you want in the store, why you don't hit your friends—by the time we got to why you can't drop your peas, well, I was dropping a few myself."

So be prepared for the amount of patience it will take to teach your children what they need to know. And put it into perspective when your children are picking up new skills, like learning to use the toilet and to dress themselves and you'll be able to praise, encourage and cheerlead them, rather than feel frustrated and worried that they'll never figure it out. You can focus on the effort and the good tries—the process—rather than thinking, "How hard can that possibly be?" The fact is, it can be pretty hard. Consider how awkward and clumsy you felt when you tried a new sport or when you started a new job. Then imagine that you're a kid and you've never mastered anything before so you don't know quite how to do it. At least as an adult you have the confidence that you have mastered other things before. You eventually learned to play basketball, so you know you'll eventually get soccer figured out, too. But your child doesn't necessarily have that knowledge or belief in himself. He has never gone to school before so how can he be sure he won't fail miserably at kindergarten? It may seem like a silly worry to you, but it's an enormous one to him. Take it seriously. Understand that your child is learning new techniques and that you and your child will both have to be patient.

Exercise

If you find yourself getting frustrated and impatient with your child's progress, try picking up a new skill yourself—something you've never done before. If you're athletic, don't pick another sport. Pick something different, like crochet or a new computer program. If you're a bookworm, sign up at your local volleyball league. Not only will learning the new skill help remind you what it's like for your children, it will take your mind off their progress for a bit. And you might end up with a fun new hobby.

22
Visualize your real parenting goals

We have many goals for our children and for ourselves as parents. But sometimes we forget what our "real" goal is. Which means we don't achieve exactly what we want to achieve.

Martial artists face this conundrum all the time, and it's never more amply illustrated than in the process of board-breaking (which isn't so much a physical exercise as a mental one). Suppose as a beginner you learn how to do a side kick and then you're instructed to break a board using the kick. The board is the target, so that seems straightforward enough, although maybe a little intimidating (won't hitting a board hurt your foot?).

The result can be predicted: You hit the board and nothing happens. That's because your strike is landing *on* the target. In order to break the board, your strike has to go *through* it. The real target is behind the board. You must aim to hit the target beyond the target. By changing your focus slightly, by trying to hit a target six inches behind the board, chances are you're going to splinter the board.

As parents, we need to look at the targets behind our targets—that is, what we're hoping to accomplish by setting the goals, rules and expectations that we set. For example, suppose you want your toddler to clean his plate at dinner. No problem—as long as he cooperates. But what happens when he doesn't? Do you punish him? You have to look at what you want to accomplish with the goal. If you think it's important not to waste food, perhaps a different strategy would work, such as making less food, or serving smaller portions and then offering seconds for people who want them. If your reasoning is that you want your child to grow up strong and healthy, find out if this is the best way to go about achieving that goal. You may learn that he'll grow perfectly fine if he decides the amount he wants to eat. If you just don't want to raise a picky eater, then perhaps you could simply offer small amounts of the different dishes and if he doesn't find any of them appealing, well, he'll just have to wait till next meal to fill up. (Trust me, no child has ever starved because his mother refused to fix him a peanut butter sandwich.)

As your children grow older, your goals and expectations for them will likewise change. And again, you'll want to consider the goal behind the goal. Suppose you want your grade-schooler to do the dishes. Well, if he does it, no problem, right? But what if he balks? Do you punish him for not doing the dishes? What if you looked at the target beyond the target? What is the purpose of having him do the dishes? Is it to teach him to be responsible? Is it to teach him that everyone must contribute to the family? Is it because you don't want to do the dishes yourself?

By understanding the target behind the target, you can formulate a plan for success. For example, if you're trying to teach him to be responsible, maybe there are other, even better, ways to do this. I know a woman who told her son that their average electric bill was $75 a month. If he could reduce the electric bill from that amount, he could pocket the difference. Imagine how he went around the house turning off the lights, finding energy-efficient ways of doing things, deciding if he really needed to have all the appliances running all the time. Lesson learned, and no need for a lot of nagging.

By focusing on the target behind the target, you can become a more effective parent.

Exercise

Consider the goals and expectations you have for your child. What is the target behind the target? Will the goal you have set help your child reach the "real" target? Many parents get into fights with their children over their messy rooms. What is the real target of a clean room? Are you teaching your children the importance of organization? Or is it that you just can't stand the sight of an unmade bed? If it's the latter, close the door and get on with your life. A messy room is not the end of the world. If it's the former, then teach organizational skills to your child beyond just picking up the mess. Help your child develop a system to prevent the mess in the first place. Make a goal of having everything in its place every night before bed so that the mess doesn't ever become too unmanageable for your child to clean up on her own.

23
Your beliefs guide your strategy in child-rearing

As a self-defense facilitator, I believe that if my students ever actually have to stand and fight, I haven't been as effective as possible—because I believe that most fights can be avoided through awareness, boundary setting, listening to intuition and being wise about whom you hang out with. So when I teach, I teach the strategies of intuition-building and boundary setting and saying, "No!"

As a parent, your beliefs should guide your strategy as well. I homeschool my daughter because I don't believe a better choice exists now where I live. It requires some compromises on my part, but it's what I believe, and so I do it. If you want your child to have strong religious beliefs, for example, then you have to consider which actions will help you reach that goal. Will you need to arrange for your child to attend religious education classes? Will you have to be sure to attend religious events regularly? Will you have to integrate religion into all aspects of your life? Of course, this doesn't guarantee your child will follow your lead, but it certainly sets the stage by giving your child a background that encourages religious belief much more than if you didn't do anything.

It may be that attending services on Sunday is sometimes inconvenient, or that tithing, which may be a practice you follow, is hard on your budget, but if you have these beliefs, your actions should reflect them.

E x e r c i s e

Remember to let your beliefs guide your strategy and actions—not what's most convenient today or what the path of least resistance might be. Create a list of your priorities—the top few things that you think are essential for your child to become a healthy, happy, productive adult—and put together an action plan that will ensure that the life you're living reflects those values.

24
Parent in public as you do in private

When I teach self-defense techniques to women, I often find that I have to encourage them not to worry about being embarrassed for using the strategies. If I say, "Get off the elevator if you don't have a good feeling about the person who just got on," someone will tell me that she'd feel foolish getting out of an elevator if a group of Hell's Angels got on instead of riding to the tenth floor with them. What if it turned out those Hell's Angels are all really nice guys after all? Wouldn't that reflect badly on her? Wouldn't she be embarrassed for making an unwarranted judgment?

But I remind them that no one ever died of embarrassment, that anyone could understand the need to protect yourself and that feeling a little foolish is certainly better than winding up shoved in a trunk somewhere.

Their self-consciousness prevents them from acting before an attack occurs—and sometimes even when an attack is under way. So I'm constantly reminding them not to worry about feeling embarrassed. And we practice all the techniques a lot so they no longer feel silly about yelling really, really loudly if the situation seems to warrant it. Over time, they build up enough confidence that they *can* risk it—they're willing to shout "No!" It doesn't embarrass them after all. They know that being willing to act will keep them safe.

As mothers, we often let self-consciousness prevent us from acting, as well. Or at least, we let it prevent us from acting as we would otherwise act. In other words, we let self-consciousness affect how we parent. Instead of parenting in public just as we do in private, we parent differently in public because we don't want to embarrass ourselves or our children. We don't want people staring at us, making mental judgments about our worth as a parent.

For instance, you're in the grocery store and your kid wants a box of sugar-coated chocolate chemicals and you say no, and he starts yelling. We have all been mightily tempted to just grab the box and shut the kid up. All right, we've all *done* it. Because we know people are watching and they're judging us. But if this is not what you would do in private, then it shouldn't be what you do in public. (This also means that what you do in private ought to be broadly acceptable in public!)

Sometimes parenting in public as we do in private also means overruling well-meaning people. If you're visiting your parents, and you correct your child and your parents say, "Oh, don't be so hard on the poor kid," your first reaction might be to back off a little. But remember, your kids need consistency. The rules need to be enforced no matter where you are. A simple remark like, "Oh, if he gets away with that, he'll soon be setting fire to the house," can help you deflect the implied criticism (that you're unnecessarily harsh) and gently remind your parents that you're the one in charge of your child.

By being confident that you're doing the right thing even when you feel self-conscious about it, you'll actually reduce how self-conscious you feel. You'll know that you're in charge and you're responsible, and it doesn't matter that other people are watching. In fact, they're probably watching you in admiration, impressed by the way you handled a sticky situation!

Exercise

Parenting in public as you do in private is much, much harder than it appears, and I know that. So the secret is to practice it a lot. All the time. Everywhere. No matter where you are and no matter who is watching. If you're home, just the two of you; if you're at your mom's house; if you're with a friend. Tell your mother or your friend that you're trying to enforce the rules and you'd appreciate their support. Talk about if afterward if you need to ("I know little Jimmy was a terror at your house and I'm sorry I had to cut our coffee time short, but I'm trying to teach him that he has to share." Or whatever). Once you train yourself to act no matter what, you'll find that you're not self-conscious at all anymore. You're just a mom doing your job.

25
Aiki, the impassive mind, creates calm mother-child relationships

Keeping a calm mind can be very helpful in dealing with our children, especially when emotions are running high. If your toddler is having tantrums, being provoked into a tantrum yourself doesn't solve the problem. If your grade-schooler is talking back to you, blowing your stack probably won't make your child more respectful. But keeping on a quiet, even keel can make all the difference in your dealings with your children and the challenges they bring you.

Martial artists call this calm, impassive mind "*aiki.*" They know that if they respond too emotionally to a situation, they will have difficulty meeting challenges. If the opponent scores a point, and the martial artist lets that demoralize her, she may lose the fight. Conversely, if she scores a point on the opponent and gets excited over it, she may be distracted or underestimate her opponent and lose the fight. So she strives for equilibrium when she faces tough challenges. She tries to keep her mind and her thoughts impassive. She will notice that her opponent scored a point, but it won't upset her. She'll recognize that she scored a point, but she won't prematurely celebrate winning the match.

In the same way, developing a calm, impassive mind can help you, as a mother, deal with everyday conflicts as well as more serious difficulties. If it's time for your preschooler to put her toys away and go to bed and she resists, being calm but firm is more likely to persuade her that she needs to do as you say than losing your temper, making threats or giving up will. Cultivating an impassive mind means that you don't respond personally when your grade-schooler is unhappy with your rules and says he hates you. He may feel that way because you're thwarting his desires, but if you remain calm and firm you will reinforce that he needs to follow your rules, and you'll recognize that his comments are made out of frustration, not hate. (Which doesn't mean that you won't be shocked and hurt the first time you hear it!)

If you can realize that most conflicts with your children are not about personality but about power, it's easier to stay more neutral and impassive when emotions are running high. You're more likely to make better choices. For instance, think about toilet training for a moment. Most parents can hardly wait until their toddlers are out of diapers. Yet they realize that they can't force their children to learn to use the toilet. Bribes and threats and cajolery won't result in a toilet-trained child. Most parents realize that this is one situation where the child has all the power. Therefore, instead of exerting strong pressure, losing your temper, or otherwise trying to use power to force a child to do what you want (become toilet trained), you realize that being calm and patient and encouraging about the process will most likely result in success. Having that impassive mind results in calmer, saner interactions with your children.

For more serious challenges, having a calm, impassive

mind contributes to your ability to solve problems and act in a crisis. Nancy Pistorius, the mother of one, recalls that her daughter was born with sleep apnea—a leading cause of sudden infant death syndrome (SIDS). When Alyssa came home from the hospital, she was hooked up to an apnea monitor. If the monitor alarm sounded in the middle of the night, Nancy had to rush to her daughter's side and make sure she was breathing. When she wasn't breathing, Nancy had to perform CPR. The stress of this situation could have been overwhelming for Nancy, but she focused on staying calm when she heard the alarm, instead of panicking. This enabled her to do what needed to be done to care for her daughter. If she had allowed her emotions—fear for her daughter, concern that she would sleep through an alarm, anxiety over performing CPR correctly every single time—to overwhelm her, she wouldn't have been as effective as a mother. But by consciously choosing to maintain a calm, healthy mind she helped her daughter weather her difficult early years to grow into a poised, happy young woman.

Exercise

Cultivating *aiki* is a conscious choice. It doesn't mean you don't or shouldn't feel emotions. It just means you take time to become calm instead of reacting (or overreacting) in the heat of the moment. You can choose *aiki* by deliberately stepping back when you feel emotions running high, taking a moment to clear your mind and taking some deep, cleansing breaths. You may also find meditating and visualization (the art of "seeing" how you want an interaction to go) to be helpful in developing *aiki*. (See Lesson #95.)

26

Persist even when you are fatigued

To build endurance, martial artists push themselves in training. They continue to train even when they feel tired and their legs weigh more than lead. They do one more throw or one more kick before stopping for rest. As time goes on, they're able to do more because they've deliberately built their endurance even though they were tired.

For parents, pushing onward even though you're tired is a time-honored art. But when I say "persist even when you are fatigued," I don't mean something like going without sleep, which most of us would agree is counterproductive. What I mean is that you don't give up just because you're in the middle of a hard spell with your child.

A simple example of this principle is when your child asks you if she can have a piece of apple pie. You tell her that she can have it as dessert after dinner. She says she wants it now. You say you told her she could have it for dessert, but not now because you don't want her to spoil her dinner. She says she's starving right this minute and dinner isn't ready yet. Now you have a choice to make: Do you stick with your "no apple pie" decision or do you give up and let her have the apple pie before she drives you nuts? Of course, we know that being consistent is key to dealing with children, and if you say "no" you have to mean it. But coming up against a really stubborn, determined child can make even the most resolute of us sigh and throw our hands up in despair. Even so, when you do that, you just encourage your child to continue to ignore the rules, argue about your decisions and increase her defiance, all because sometimes this behavior gets her exactly what she wants. By sticking to your original choice ("no apple pie"), you're actually making it easier on yourself down the road, because your child will learn that you mean what you say.

While most of us can imagine being firm and consistent during specific instances—such as the apple pie conflict described above—it's harder when you must persist day in and day out for longer periods of time. But that's often what it takes to deal with a chronic behavior problem. You need to commit to being determined and persistent up front. Take, for example, the comparatively common behavior problem of a toddler or preschooler hitting other people when he's mad, upset or frustrated. Yes, you can tell him that it's not nice to hit other people but having that conversation one time probably isn't going to solve the problem—it's going to be a process of reinforcing your rules (no biting) over a period of time. You'll have to pay attention to what sets him off and, when you can, intervene before the hitting actually occurs. You'll have to make sure he apologizes for his behavior and remind him of the rules. If the behavior continues, you'll have to decide if he should be punished when he does it, and how he should be punished. And then you'll have to continue policing his actions when you'd much rather sit with the other mothers at the playgroup and have a cup of coffee. But this constant, steady persistence will eventually get the job done.

For most of the challenges we face as mothers, there is no magical elixir, no quick-fix solution. The job is to be patient and consistent for a long, long time, even when you feel incredibly tired and just want to give up. But by persisting, you will begin to feel much more capable of handling the behavior problems that crop up now and then. They become easier to correct, and you'll have the confidence that you can do it. If you persist, you're more likely to get the result you want.

Exercise

Get the support you need to persist even when fatigued. When Jessica had a specific behavior problem that exhausted all my efforts to correct it, I knew I needed to do more than just keep trying. I didn't even know if I was handling the behavior in an effective way. So by consulting with others and getting feedback when I put their ideas into practice, I was able to feel supported and encouraged as I tried to change the behavior. By asking for encouragement and support—and, if necessary, professional help—you'll be able to handle the challenges and continue to parent effectively even through tough times.

27
Master the present

One of the delights of training in the martial arts is slipping into the *dobok* or *gi* (the martial arts uniform) and walking onto the mat and focusing all your attention on what you're doing right this minute. When you train, all you can do is think about the kick you're performing, or the *kata* (form) you're doing. You can't really worry about the nasty thing your boss said today or that scary presentation you have to give tomorrow. There's no room for that. All you can do is focus on what you're doing. It's a wonderful form of physical meditation.

Focusing on the present—on what you're doing right now—can be difficult as a mother. There's so much to plan for and so much to do that it's easy to get distracted. And, let's face it, sometimes being stuck in the house with three kids under five on a snowy day can make you long for the time to come when they'll all be at college. But as mom Gina Binole says, "Don't wish your kids' lives away. So often mothers say things like, 'I can't wait till they sleep through the night.' 'I can't wait till they eat solid food.' 'I can't wait till they're walking.' I tell friends to savor every moment. Time flies at a furious pace all on its own, without you pushing it along."

By mastering the present—focusing on being present-oriented and fully living in the present, you'll be able to enjoy the experience of being a mother. Too often we plan to do something with our children tomorrow. We'll have more time for reading books before bed once we start our new job. We'll be able to go to the park next week after we're finished painting the bathroom even though the sun is shining today. But if you can instead focus on the present—and be present—you can be satisfied that you're doing your job as a loving, effective parent.

By savoring the moment—as many of them as you can—you'll experience the joy that everyday moments can bring. By training your mind to focus on what you're doing, you're less likely to get distracted and more likely to enjoy present opportunities. If you're in too much of a hurry, you overlook so much that will be gone so soon—the grin on your two-year-old's face, the way your one-year-old scrunches up her nose when she smells dinner, the laugh of your five-year-old as the kitten's whiskers tickle her. If you're unfocused, worried about everything that needs to be done and constantly on the go, go, go, you'll miss the real pleasures of motherhood.

Exercise

Be all here. Choose to be mindful of what you're doing at the moment. You're reading, breathing in and out, perhaps sipping a cup of tea. Experience the moment. What do you hear? What do you smell? What does the book feel like in your hands? Are you sitting or standing or perhaps soaking in the tub? Are you comfortable? Is the light good?

When you want to remind yourself to focus on the moment—when you're feeling harried and distracted—find a quiet spot (the bathroom?) and take a moment to center yourself and state your intention. ("By taking a moment to center myself, I'll experience the moment and feel less distracted and overwhelmed.") Place your hands over your abdomen, where your chi originates. Take a deep breath and focus on that chi energy. Exhale the stress and frustration, inhale the calm serenity that will help you stay in the moment.

28

Growth as a mother occurs
when you keep trying

Mothers grow as they keep trying. Since you don't get a pass from the demands of mothering—you have to show up even if you have the flu—you have to accept that sometimes you're going to be imperfect. If you feel today you weren't the most perfect mother, well, tomorrow you'll have the opportunity to try again. Recognize that as a mother, you're in for bad days. That's because you're working twenty-four hours a day, seven days a week, all year long.

There's more to mothering than showing up, of course. If you can accept that there are going to be difficulties, and sometimes you're not going to shine so bright, then you can learn from the challenges you face. Yet there's no room for growth or change if you decide you're a terrible mother and that's it. Remember, you're not a failure until you give up.

When a martial artist begins training, she is shown how to do some basic techniques. If she doesn't do the technique correctly on the first try, has she failed? Of course not. No one expects her to get it right on the first time or the fiftieth time or even the five thousandth time. As long as she keeps practicing and she keeps trying, she is not failing, she is not a failure. If she gives up, *then* she's a failure.

When Dr. Sally Goldberg's daughter was born with Down syndrome, she knew she'd face some difficult days—and she also knew she had to keep trying no matter what. So when setbacks occurred or she didn't handle a problem as well as she would have liked, she repeated her mantra: "What happens when you fall down? You pick yourself up and keep going." Invent a mantra like that for yourself, to help inspire persistence and courage. Mine is telling the universe, "Thank you for everything. I have no complaints whatsoever"—a mantra I borrowed from a much wiser woman.

The idea that you're not a failure if you keep trying is also an important concept to communicate to our children. If we're able to convince our children to keep trying no matter what happens, we rob the idea of failure of much of its power. It's not something to be afraid of. Too often fear of failure prevents our children from pursuing activities and hobbies that interest them. They think if they don't master something right away, they never will. But the ability to keep trying is a gift—an important one.

One of the ways to encourage this attitude is to not use the word "failure" yourself. It's also important for you to show persistence to your children. If you keep trying when something doesn't work out the first time, your children will see that and be more likely to follow your example. If you give up trying to fix the kitchen sink after the first attempt, what do you communicate to your child? If you never seem to try something new, maybe your child thinks you're afraid of failing, too.

E x e r c i s e

Encourage your very young children to keep trying. Let your preschool-age children figure out how to draw a pony or a person. Let them decide how they're going to cure the boredom that sometimes sets in by Saturday afternoon. You can support them but you don't have to do the task for them.

For an older child, you can encourage persistence by joining him or her in an activity. Take up something that both of you might like to do: Learn the guitar, take ballet, practice yoga. (Of course, respect your child's wishes if she'd rather drop dead than see you in a leotard.) By doing things together, you can encourage each other, your child can egg you on and you can show how success is achieved—by never giving up.

29
Know your child's most pressing needs and desires

In the martial arts, a vital point is a vulnerable area (the nose, the groin) that you would target in an attacker and that you would protect on yourself. Damaging a vital point inflicts a lot of pain and distress.

In mothering, the vital points for your child are the needs and desires he has that will shape the adult he becomes. If you can meet the most vital of these, your child will thrive. For example, all children need nutritious food, plenty of exercise and lots of love. Those are vital points. Without them, your child will suffer. And all children have certain pressing desires—for example, the desire to have friends to play with, interesting toys and books to interact with and the opportunity to make their own choices, at least now and then.

It's important for a mother to understand the vital points in her child's life. What are the most important things for the child, both now and in terms of her future success? What are his most pressing needs and desires? While some of the vital points are the same for all children (love, good food), others vary from child to child.

To determine the vital points for your child, you need to tap into your intuition. Sometimes you just "know" when something is vitally important to your child. But you also need to be able to see your child objectively. One of my colleagues, who teaches hearing-impaired children, tells me that some of the parents refuse to learn sign language to communicate with their children, because they simply won't believe that their children are disabled in this way—even though the objective evidence shows that the child cannot hear, or cannot hear very well. And I'm told that these parents otherwise appear very loving and attentive toward their children. But being in a state of denial about what your child needs does not help your child thrive.

As author Jane Adams points out, "It's a rare parent who can see his or her child clearly and objectively. At a school board meeting I attended, the only definition of a gifted child on which everyone in the audience could agree was 'mine.'"

Even so, making the effort to see your child clearly and objectively—although with compassion—can help you discover the most vital needs for her. If your two-year-old isn't saying any words yet, recognize that she may be developing just fine and will eventually start talking, but consult with a physician and perhaps a speech therapist anyway. Don't dismiss concerns you have about your child. And don't let others make you feel foolish for having them. Yes, all children develop at their own pace. But sometimes a problem develops that can be treated successfully—and if you catch it early enough, you can often reduce the impact it will have on your child over the long term.

In the same way, if you can identify a few of your child's most pressing desires and meet them, you'll help your child thrive more than if you had fulfilled dozens of lesser desires. The vital points don't always have to be long-term, big desires. A few weeks ago, my niece Alexis spent the greater part of dinner at a restaurant squatting by the window next to our table and watching a bug make its way across the sidewalk. Her mother didn't force her to sit down and eat. Another mother might have, but Beth felt it was just fine for Alexis to fulfill her interest in watching the world around her, and she simply brought Alexis's meal home in a takeout carton. If she had demanded that Alexis sit down and eat her meal and ignore the bug, Alexis would have been upset and frustrated, and no amount of animal crackers (her favorite) would have made her feel any better. In the same way, if your child badly wants to learn to play the guitar, giving him lessons and renting or buying a guitar for him is worth far more to him than if you had spent three times as much money lavishing him with dirt bikes and computer games.

Sometimes we feel that our children's desires and interests are too single-minded and we worry that our children will grow up "lopsided." For instance, if your daughter constantly has her nose in a book, your inclination might be to shoo her outside to play for a while despite her objections. Of course children do need to run and play, but at the same time, you could be communicating the message that your child's interests are absurd or unimportant.

Instead of dismissing or trying to curtail your child's interests, build on them. If your child is constantly reading books, find out what she's reading about. Is she in the middle of the Laura Ingalls Wilder series about being a pioneer girl? Then maybe you can encourage her to make a pioneer meal for everyone to share one evening, or camp in the backyard like Laura camped on the prairie, or make a play about an event that happened in Laura's life. All of these will get your child's nose out of the book for a while but also show that you want to support and encourage her interests.

When Jessica watched the Rudolph the Red-Nosed Reindeer movie on a computer DVD, she fell in love with Rudolph. She wanted to watch the show fifteen times a day. But I didn't want to let her sit in front of the computer all day long. Instead of just telling her she couldn't watch the show, I bought her a book about Rudolph that we read several times a day (and took with us everywhere). We counted reindeers and talked about what they were and where they lived and what the North Pole was. We sang the Rudolph song every night before bed—sometimes three or four times—and I repeated the lines until she could memorize them. We drew pictures of Rudolph. One of my sisters found a Rudolph coloring book that was treasured until it fell into tatters. We looked him up on the Internet and found out all about him. For Christmas, I found her a Rudolph toy that said a few phrases when you squeezed its ears, and a couple of miniatures of the other characters in the movie (and wouldn't you know? I wouldn't have needed to give her anything else). Eventually her interest in Rudolph faded, but during the months in which she loved him dearly, we found many ways to incorporate him into our lives and learn from him.

By finding ways to identify and help your child fulfill his most pressing needs and desires, you can help him grow, learn and thrive.

Exercise

When you're not certain how important a request is to a child—and thus not sure how "vital" it is—find out how much they're willing to give up for it or how much they're willing to put into it. For instance, if your toddler wants the expensive purple ketchup, is he willing to put back the package of stickers in order to get it? If your older child wants a new skateboard, instead of simply saying, "We can't afford it," find out what your child is willing to do to get it. Will he save up half the money? Will he sell his old skateboard and put the money toward the new? Will he do extra chores around the house? Often you'll find that it's not worth it to the child—and that's your answer. You shouldn't have to put in extra hours at the office to afford the cool new Nike shoes if your kid isn't willing to take on some extra responsibility, too. On the other hand, sometimes he's thrilled to get a chance to work toward something important to him, and that's your answer, too.

By teaching your child to make these types of decisions, you're reinforcing a skill that will be crucial for him later in life—he'll be able to learn for himself what he really wants by choosing the option that will give him the most satisfaction out of a multiplicity of choices, and he'll be able to make value decisions, taking into consideration the amount of work, time and energy that will have to go into getting it. So when he's an adult, he can decide if he really wants the Porsche so much that he's willing to live in a dinky apartment on the bad side of town in order to afford it, and he'll be able to determine if buying only designer suits is worth the extra work he has to put in to pay for them.

30

Understand the nature of yin-yang

Many Taoist beliefs underlie the principles of the martial arts. One of these is the concept of yin-yang—the idea that the universe is made up of conflicting yet harmonious elements that work together. You can't have one without the other—no night without day, no darkness without light.

You can see this principle at work in your own life as a mother, too. There's an ebb and flow to your parenting and to your child's needs. Sometimes it seems that your child is only causing trouble—getting into arguments, ignoring the rules, teasing the cat. Other times, you couldn't hope for a more pleasant companion. You enjoy playing games together, going on outings, laughing over cartoons. Sometimes you'll get along with your children remarkably well. Other times it's like pulling teeth to talk without arguing.

Understanding and accepting the cycle of yin-yang helps you in your parenting. If you want to think of this as "phases," that's fine, too. It's the idea that sometimes it's smooth sailing and sometimes it's stormy seas, and often you can't do much about it. By understanding and accepting the nature of yin-yang, you're not caught by surprise when a shift occurs and you don't overreact to it.

Of course, you don't want to ignore warning signs or dismiss real trouble as just a phase your child is going through. But you can realize that this difficult patch won't last forever and you'll just have to do the best you can to get through it.

I've discovered that everything has its own cycle, even chronic illnesses like the one Jessica has. There are times when she has few problems followed by periods when she has a lot of problems. Understanding this means that I don't sink into despair when she has a bad patch. I have faith we'll get through it. And when she has a good period, I enjoy it and take advantage of it, knowing it won't last forever. I remember to value the good times.

Exercise

Keep a journal of your experiences with your child. As you have ups and downs, record how you feel, what's happening and when and how the bad times resolved. Doing so helped me identify times when it was more likely that Jessica would have conflict with me (whenever we changed her schedule unexpectedly). It's also a reference tool that you can look back on to encourage yourself— you will see the light at the end of the tunnel. You may also be able to spot patterns, which can help you head off bad times.

31

Pick your battles wisely

Martial artists are taught to avoid using physical techniques if they can. They're trained to defuse tense situations, walk away when they can and figure out what's worth fighting for. Obviously, it's not worth risking being injured or even killed if the mugger just grabs your purse. Nothing you own is worth that. On the other hand, if you or someone you love was in physical danger and you couldn't get away from it, then of course you would stand and fight.

Likewise, it's important for mothers to choose what they think is important enough to create rules for, and to what extent they want to push the fight. As my colleague Suzanne says, "Pick your battles. You can't win them all. You shouldn't win them all. When I was wise enough to follow it, it worked. I still follow it with my grandkids. With my children, I open then close my mouth without saying a word. I don't offer advice unless it's a big issue or I really think they are making a mistake."

For instance, you may expect that your children get good grades, and therefore set a rule about getting a minimum grade in each class. Another mother might decide that the important thing is for her child to put forth her best effort, not that she necessarily scores high on an arbitrary grading system. And yet another mother might believe it's more important for her child to develop a passion for and thorough knowledge of a certain field, so if he gets a "C" in social studies while demonstrating an amazing aptitude in math, she'll be perfectly happy. What's important—and to what extent it is important—varies from family to family.

My sister Beth says, "My rules are based on, is it dangerous? If it is, I call it a 'rule.' Like holding my hand when we cross the street. She knows that's a rule, and she has to follow it. I'll give her a warning—'That's the rule, Alexis'—and if she ignores me, then we stop what we're doing. If it's just obnoxious behavior, I don't give it nearly the same amount of weight and attention. I tell her 'no,' try to distract her, go outside with her, something simple like that."

Children do need the authority and structure of rules

about their behavior. But it's important not to lump all less-than-perfect behavior into one category. Not picking up your toys isn't worth fighting over in the same way as not sticking forks in the electrical outlets. By setting rules, we show our children we care about them and we care what happens to them. But if we create too many rules, the child can easily feel he just can't win and may simply ignore them all. Plus, all of the constant conflict generated by too many rules does not lead to happy and harmonious homes.

Exercise

Consciously consider what rules of behavior your child should have, taking into consideration that the rules and expectations will change as your children grow. Very young children of course can't make decisions for themselves, so you have to protect them by making sure your home is childproofed and that they're constantly supervised. Toddlers can understand simple rules, like "don't run into the street" and "don't pull the dog's tail." Whether they'll comply is another issue—and since you'll have to enforce the rules, it's best to limit them to the most important ones.

Older children can understand more sophisticated rules, as they can understand cause-and-effect or consequences. But instead of trying to legislate all aspects of their lives, create a few overarching rules that encompass a variety of desired behaviors. For instance, "Be courteous" covers a multitude of behaviors, from not fighting with siblings to not talking back to parents. Explain that you value courtesy and expect your child to be courteous at all times and set out the consequences if it doesn't happen. In the same way, instead of having a lot of rules about "no watching television until your homework is done," which turns you into a cop, you can have a basic rule of "you must maintain a C average" (or whatever is important to you). You can encourage your child to develop good habits such as doing homework before watching television, but you don't have to police every action. If your child doesn't get his homework done, and it affects his grade, he will ultimately face the music when he brings home a D on his report card.

32

Focus on the Way

The "destination" of our lives is death. Yet we'd miss out on the whole purpose of living if we focused on the destination rather than the journey. Sometimes, when you're dealing with your kids, and your spouse and work, you can find yourself focusing on the destination: Your kids are grown and out of the house and you're retired in the Bahamas somewhere. But if you do that, you miss out on the entire point of having children. By emphasizing the journey, you can find the right actions for each step of the way and you'll find you grow and change just as your children do.

The principle of following the Tao (the Way) underlies most martial arts. The Tao is thought to be a natural, simple, relaxed approach to life, in which you concentrate on internal matters, not on external achievements, such as money, fame or praise. When I teach martial artists, I see that some of them don't understand this. Some students seem focused only on achieving their black belts, yet the black belt is not the point of training. Few of these students ever make it, because it's a long, hard road and you have to be committed. And the only way to be committed is to be focused on the journey, to love the journey and to find the journey rewarding, to grow and develop as you move along the path. Otherwise, what's the point? Some of these students do make it to black belt and then they never come back for more training. They reached their destination . . . and they still missed the point.

So you need to focus on the journey, on the Way, on the process of raising your children. And if you can do that in a natural, simple and relaxed way, in which you concentrate on the eternal things—the things that truly matter—you and your children will be calmer, more fulfilled and happier. If you concern yourself with raising your children in the way that you think is most important and are not concerned with the values of the outside world, and if you try to keep your family life simple and harmonious, you'll reap the rewards of having focused on the right things.

When my friends Bob and Tess began to focus on nurturing their family, they decided to rethink their careers and agreed to simplify their lives. Tess, the primary breadwinner, quit her job to spend more time at home. They gave away or sold much of what they owned and moved into a smaller house. Eventually, Tess trained to become a spiritual leader, which is what she does now. It hasn't always been easy, but because they're focused on what they do want—more time with their kids—the tough times never seem that bad.

Focus on the Way—on helping your child grow into an adult who understands that peace and happiness come from inside, not from how big his house is or how fancy his car.

Remember that there's no other child like yours. Focus on the process of discovering this child you have and on the process of guiding her to adulthood with your support and encouragement. By recognizing that the inner matters more than the outer, by staying in the moment, and enjoying the journey rather than keeping your sights on the destination, you'll create an atmosphere of harmony and peace.

When your toddler pulls off his diaper and runs around the house naked, shrieking with delight while you try to catch him, you'll laugh instead of scold him. When your grade-schooler comes home with torn jeans because he just discovered he can climb all the way to the top of the tree, you'll recognize that the accomplishment is more significant than having to patch the jeans. When your teenager gets her nose pierced, instead of grounding her for three months, you'll focus on the fact that she's a happy, generous kid who does a pretty good job in school and doesn't cause you a lot of grief.

33
Mothering includes disappointments and complications

Motherhood isn't as simple as we might like to believe. You don't just have your baby, enjoy her lovely childhood, shepherd her confidently through adolescence and then see her off to adulthood before taking a well-deserved rest. There will be plenty of detours in between.

When martial artists begin training, they find that they learn a lot in the first few months. They pick up many new skills, become more confident, get more fit. So sometimes they're not prepared when a roadblock appears. They hit a plateau. They have trouble learning a new technique. They get an injury. They can't remember their old form. They blow a test. They discover the Way is not always straight. You don't just go from white belt to black belt with no detours in between.

Just like these martial artists, some mothers seem to think their children should be able to just go from point A (babyhood) to point B (adulthood) with no complications. Many of us think that would be ideal. But it's not ideal. What would anyone learn from that? How could an adult cope with adulthood if there had never been a rough spot in childhood?

Which is not to say that you shouldn't try to keep your life complication-free if you can. Just that you're not going to be able to avoid all the complications. Your ten-month-old is going to figure out how to unlatch the baby gate. Your toddler is going to fall off the chair she's climbing on (even though you've told her ten times not to). Your grade-schooler is going to take on the bully himself and get a black eye.

And consider that children learn from their mistakes. If they don't have to work hard and be disappointed now and then, they'll never learn the satisfaction of mastering a skill. Watching your child bobble the final out of the ball game, allowing the opposing team to score four runs and win the game might be hard, but imagine how it feels next year when your child hits the game-winning home run. You wouldn't appreciate it nearly as much if you hadn't seen your child make her share of mistakes, and neither would your child.

As a mother, you'll also make your share of mistakes. You'll yell at your kids for breaking the vase when the dog did it, make them cry without meaning to, forget to take them to the park this weekend like you promised. You'll respond less than heroically to a crisis, faint at the sight of blood and let the baby go two weeks without a bath. The list of ways you'll be disappointed in your performance is practically endless.

Bad days happen, complications arise, and if you're prepared for them—not afraid of them—you'll find yourself handling the challenges with grace and serenity, or at least with more grace and serenity than you would have had if you really thought it could all be simple and straightforward.

Exercise

Think back to when you were a child. Remember a time when something difficult happened and yet you overcame it. Maybe you failed a test and had to tell your parents but you eventually went on to do pretty well in the subject. Or you asked someone to the prom and he said no and you went with your friends and had a good time anyway. Weren't these complications disappointing at the time, but haven't they also helped you become the person you are today?

Disappointments we have with our children also make us better mothers. We grow through facing these difficulties—including our own failings—and learning to handle the complications thrown our way.

34

Seek to be connected
to other mothers

Martial arts don't exist in a vacuum and neither do martial artists. They know they're part of a larger community. They're connected to other martial artists everywhere. Their art has been handed down for generations and will be handed down for generations more. Most important, martial artists are connected to other students training in their school. A martial artist cannot become a martial artist without these connections. Without training partners—people with whom she practices the techniques, applying them, seeing how they work against another person—she can never reach her full potential as a martial artist. Having training partners is like having your own team—they help you and you help them. Because you work together, everyone wins.

In the same way, it's important to recognize your place in the community of mothers. Of course, you have many demands on your time and connecting with other people may not be high on your list of priorities. But staying connected with other mothers helps you through the tough times.

I remember when Jessica was very small, just a few months old, she was in the hospital being treated for status epilepticus—her seizures wouldn't stop. I had pulled down one side of the crib so I could rest my hand on her tummy, and I was sitting in a chair by the bed and I was very, very tired and very, very worried. I laid my head on the mattress and could feel the blanket beneath my cheek. And suddenly it struck me that a whole line of other mothers had been in this room and had put their cheek on this blanket and worried about their baby. I wasn't alone—all of them were here with me. It was an enormously strengthening moment for me. I felt comforted. I felt like these mothers were telling me I would handle this, and everything would be all right.

I didn't know these mothers personally, but I knew they were there. And that is a powerful connection. Whatever you have been through, are going through, are struggling with—are celebrating!—you're never alone. There are other mothers who have been there before and who will come after.

As mothers, we sometimes forget that we need training partners, too. We need people who help us become better mothers. We need people who give us feedback, people who support us on our journey, people who cheer for our successes, people who help us through the tough times.

Ann Douglas, the author of *The Mother of All Pregnancy Books*, says, "Understand that the physical demands of mothering are the easy part. It's the emotional demands that can flatten you. So make a point of putting your support team in place right from day one—other moms who are prepared to step in and pinch hit when you need a break. Mothering was never intended to be a solo sport, after all."

Get your support team in place. It's never too late—even if your kid is already sixteen. Find other mothers who will be your "training partners." In return, you'll be there for them. Develop these relationships by joining mother groups, getting online, networking with other people in your shoes. And remember that you're not a failure or less than perfect for not being able to do it all on your own. Having training partners is essential to your success.

35

Doubt and worry cloud the mind

Worry and doubt, whenever they show up, can cloud your mind and make it difficult to do what needs to be done and to make good choices. While worry and doubt can alert you to potential dangers, they are not useful long-term emotions to have. Yes, bad things can happen to your children, but if all you do is worry about them, you're creating a negative and tense climate, and you're not doing anything to keep your children safer.

Look at it this way: If the warrior doubted she could defeat the attacker, chances are she'd be right. If you're worried about your opponent and doubt your abilities, it's hard to make the right choices. It's hard to give the commitment and effort needed to defeat the opponent, even if you're perfectly capable of doing so.

Worry and doubt are best acknowledged, then set aside in order to take appropriate action. If you're worried about your child's fever, take a deep breath and call the doctor. If you try to take action while under the cloud of worry and doubt, you may not be as effective. If you're not calm and coherent when you call the doctor to express concern over your child's fever, it will be difficult for the doctor to help you. If you don't dismiss the doubt and worry, but let them dominate your thoughts, you may not even take action. If you're so worried about your child's fever that all you can do is wring your hands, you're not taking appropriate action.

If you have a cause for worry, recognize it, then act on it. Put it aside once you've done so. If you can't do anything about your worry, just put it aside. When the worry intrudes, don't dwell on it. Turn to something else. But take whatever action you can with a clear mind, not a worried one.

For example, suppose a friend took her preschooler and yours to the park to give you a break. They promised to be back by three p.m. and now it's four o'clock and they still haven't come home. You can imagine all sorts of terrible scenarios, can't you? Your child fell off the slide and was rushed to the hospital and the next call you get will be from the pediatric neurosurgeon asking for permission to operate. Or your friend got into an accident on the way home from the park and ditto. Or a madman with a gun abducted everyone. So you can pace the floor and get increasingly worried, or you can take action. You can call your friend's cell phone. (Maybe she just lost track of time.) You can walk or drive to the park to see if you can find them (leaving a note at home in case they return while you're gone). You can decide to give them another half hour before you do anything. Any of these choices is reasonable. But you have to make the choice, and having made it, put all the fear and worry out of your mind so you can act effectively.

By letting your worry get the better of you, you're likely to act in ways that you wouldn't otherwise do. Suppose your friend forgot her watch and did just lose track of time. If you're worried sick about your child, when they come swinging happily up the walk, you're likely to start yelling at your friend about how inconsiderate she is and how worried you were—and end up in an ugly, unproductive fight. But if you remain calm, you can point out that you were growing a bit concerned, she can explain herself, and next time, you can make sure she has her watch with her before they head out the door.

Doubt can also be disabling. It can make it impossible for you to make decisions or to act on them. You would like to stay at home to be with your children but you doubt you can afford it. You'd like to go back to work but you doubt anyone will hire you. You'd like to make a more flexible work arrangement but you doubt your boss will let you. As you can see, you're not actually finding out if any of this is true. You're just paralyzing yourself with doubt.

E x e r c i s e

When you feel worry and doubt, take action. Say, "Thank you for alerting me to that," to your worries and doubt, and then act. If you're worried about your daughter's temperature, call the doctor, take her to the urgent-care facility, or decide that you're not going to worry about it unless it reaches 105 degrees. Then follow through.

36

Teach the consequences

It's important to teach our children the consequences of their actions. If we constantly protect them when they make bad decisions, they don't learn to take responsibility for themselves. Of course, as a mother, you have to protect your young children from the most serious consequences—you don't let your child run out into the street and say, well, if he gets hit by a car, he'll learn not to run out into the street. It's a matter of gradually introducing the consequences for their actions. If he leaves his toys scattered all over the living room floor, and someone accidentally steps on one and breaks it, that's a consequence. If he feeds all the strawberries to the dog, then there's no strawberry pie for dessert, and that's a consequence.

In much the same way, the beginning martial artist learns the consequences of her actions right away—but in a controlled, safe setting. For example, she is taught how to block a kick. If she doesn't do the block correctly, the teacher doesn't say, "Wow! Fabulous block!" The teacher taps her with the kick. The consequence isn't serious, but the beginner sees that she needs to do the technique differently to be successful. Maybe she needs to do it more powerfully or from a different starting position. But the teacher isn't doing the student any favors if the student never learns the consequences. The student will think her block is just fine when in fact it's not—something that could lead to a more serious consequence down the road.

My sister Michelle, who is an elementary school teacher and mother of two, says, "Let your kids fail early in life so they can learn responsibility when the stakes are not as high as when they are teenagers. For example, when your ten-year-old forgets her lunch or homework, don't drop what you are doing and run it up to school for her. She will not starve if she misses lunch for one day and she will not lose any chance of going to college because of a few missed assignments in fourth or fifth grade. My two children are now organized and remember what to bring to school better than I do. The best thing is that when they do something stupid, I can sympathize with them, but because I do not rescue them, the burden for dealing with the consequences is on their shoulders not mine. I do not feel the stress of being responsible to make everything better for them."

Although it can be difficult to watch your children bear the consequences of their actions, you're doing them a kindness in the long run—because they'll be able to handle the more difficult challenges of adulthood.

Exercise

Realize that teaching your children about consequences is an important part of their growing-up process. Resist the temptation to step in and straighten everything out for them. Commiserate with them but don't fix everything. Help them think up ways to prevent recurrences, but don't solve the problem for them. Let them figure that out themselves. When my friend Julie's six-year-old daughter Chloe came home from school and told her mother that the she and her best friend had gotten into a fight, Julie was tempted to call the other mother to find out what had happened and try to smooth things over. But she resisted doing so. Instead, she sat down with Chloe and they made up a list of things that Chloe could do to rebuild her friendship. Chloe contributed lots of good ideas, such as apologizing, offering to play with her friend at recess and finding a new friend if her old friend decided to stay mad. Chloe felt much better when she realized she could take responsibility for what had happened and try to fix it.

37
Chi overcomes obstacles

Martial artists believe that their chi, or life energy, can help them perform difficult tasks. We've talked about how chi contributes creative energy for dealing with child-rearing issues and that it's important to replenish your chi (see Lesson #2).

But chi can also be used to help you overcome obstacles and get through difficulties. It can help you focus on solving a problem. It can help you relax when faced with a difficulty. It can help you feel energized and able to combat any problem. And it can feed your creativity so you can come up with an unusual solution to your problem.

By summoning your chi, you can clear your mind and give yourself energy to cope with a problem. For instance, suppose you're having trouble getting your child to sleep in her own bed at night, all night (a very common problem). You decide to be firm and get her ready for bed, tuck her in, sing her a song, turn off the light and leave the room. When she comes out to go to the bathroom, you send her back to bed as soon as she's done. When she decides she needs a drink of water, you give her a sip and send her back to bed. Now it's quiet for a while and after the news you go to bed—only to be awakened an hour later by a little voice outside your bedroom lamenting, "Mama, I had a bad dream!" Well, you're tired; if you let her get into bed you'll be able to get back to sleep and you won't wake up exhausted in the morning. But you've made a decision, and you should stick to it. So take a moment to tap into your chi. Get out of bed, reassure your daughter and send her to back to bed. Expect that she'll be back in a few minutes. Take another deep breath and send her back to bed. In the morning, when you wake up tired because of your interrupted sleep, spend a few moments in quiet meditation, drawing on your chi to help energize you throughout the day. By sticking to your determination, you'll ensure that soon everyone will be sleeping peacefully through the night. But if you let your lack of energy overcome your good sense, you'll continue to deal with the same problem in the future.

This is just one scenario where you can tap into your chi to help overcome a problem. But how do you find your chi? How do you tap into it? Your chi is centered in your abdomen, near your navel. To feel this location, place your hand against your abdomen, take a deep breath, then breathe out using "fogging" breath—as if you were blowing on your glasses to clean them or steaming up a cold window. Do you feel your muscles tighten when you do this? That's where your chi is. Think of your womb as the source of this creative energy.

When you're faced with a difficult task, or need to summon some creativity, remember where your chi is located. Focus on drawing it up into the rest of your body. Feel it flow out your limbs, giving you strength and energy. Visualize the creative center of your chi feeding out energy for you to do what needs to be done.

Exercise

You can summon your chi through breathing exercises. When things get a little crazy, just find a quiet corner, close your eyes, breathe in slowly as you count to ten, then breathe out. As you breathe out, visualize breathing out all the negative energy. Breathe in all the good, positive energy from the world around you—the energy that you'll be able to use to cope with your difficulty, overcome an obstacle or solve a problem.

38

The wise woman is single-minded

The wise woman—the wise mother—is single-minded. That doesn't mean that she can raise only one child, must pay no attention to her husband and cannot work outside the home. That would be a little too single-minded. Our lives are much more complex than that. Being single-minded means that the wise woman focuses on the important things, when they are important, and disregards the rest. She doesn't worry about the stock plan when her child is in the hospital. This doesn't mean the stock plan won't at some point be important for her to pay attention to. Being single-minded is about focusing on what's important *when* it's important.

When the martial artist faces an opponent in the sparring ring, she focuses on one thing: winning the match. She does not wonder about who the cute guy in the third row is. She probably doesn't even see or hear him; she is focused on the opponent and on winning the match. This focus, this single-minded attention, is crucial for the warrior, the martial artist, to succeed in her endeavors. Once the match is over, now she can wonder who the cute guy in the third row is.

The wise woman is single-minded in the same way. She decides what is important and discards those things that are unimportant. I know some mothers, for instance, who, feeling pressed for time, give up volunteer activities to spend more time with their children. That's a legitimate action to take, and the type of thing a single-minded wise woman would do. If one child is having difficulties in school, then it's wise to focus on helping that child. When the problem improves, focus can shift elsewhere.

We tend to clutter up our days with lots of things going on all the time. But being scattered, unfocused and distracted makes us less effective in the roles that are important to us. When I got divorced and knew that I was going to have to scramble to make a living as a freelance writer, I got rid of my television—gave it away to a friend. This is because I love television and would watch it every evening when my time would be better spent working, playing with Jessica, catching up with friends or doing a task around the house. Getting rid of this distraction has helped me be a more single-minded mother.

Multitasking and now hypertasking have become badges of honor. We think that by talking on the phone while answering our e-mail while talking to our colleague in the next cubicle, we're being efficient and getting a lot done. But what we're doing is handling three things badly instead of one thing competently. Choose your most important priorities and get those done. The rest can wait.

Like money, you have only a certain amount of time to spend doing what needs to be done. So create a time budget (just as you might create a financial budget) and allocate your resources accordingly. Consider what's important to you right now and sketch out the number of hours it takes you to do your various tasks. Remember to include transportation time, downtime, lost minutes while you're standing in line. For example, working a 9-to-5 job doesn't take up eight hours a day. There's a commute, there's the time you spend getting ready to go, there's the time you spend on evenings and weekends finishing up projects you didn't get done during the day, there's the time you spend shopping for professional clothing and attending professional conferences and association meetings.

What else goes into your budget? You're probably responsible for household chores, taking care of the children and visiting your parents now and then. You probably like to see your friends once in a while and of course you have to bring your kids to soccer practice. Map all of this out in your budget. Yeah, no wonder you never have ten minutes to yourself.

Now identify with a highlighter or with an asterisk those items that are the most important—going to work, being with your kids. What can you eliminate or pare down? Maybe instead of doing all the household chores yourself, you could delegate. A friend of mine hires a caterer to provide her with meals for the entire week. The cost is about the same as what she'd spend at the grocery store, and on takeout, fast food and restaurant meals that she'd otherwise rely on throughout the week—plus she feels good that her family is getting good, nutritious home-cooked (well, pretty close) meals. Since I work from home and am a writer, I have to do a lot of little errands like run to the post office several times a week, make copies, update databases and more. So I hired someone to do those things, freeing up at least five or six hours of my time each week. I can spend that time earning money, or I can spend that time with Jessica. Either way, it's a better deal for me.

By seeing how you spend your time and making an effort to allocate your time to the most important things in your life, you'll be a wise woman indeed!

39
Play it smart

One of the principles I teach my self-defense students is that they can follow all the "stay safe" advice they read in the newspaper and on the Internet and they could still get attacked. This is not meant to frighten them, but to point out that the most important skill they can develop isn't the habit of locking the doors, looking under the bed or asking for escorts when leaving the office after dark; it's the habit of being smart, of relying on their intelligence, creativity and cleverness to get out of a self-defense situation.

Jennie Phipps, a mother and writer in Detroit, says, "My mother never told me to be careful—she always told me to be smart. And that's what I told my own children as soon as they were able to venture out of my sight. Being careful won't keep them out of trouble, but being smart might."

While your instinct might be to keep your children

safely tucked away at home (I know that's mine!), it's not realistic or desirable. Children do need to get out into the world, to explore it, learn to handle it and otherwise become fully functioning adults. If you just tell them to be careful—even if you give them advice like "don't take candy from strangers"—you're not preparing them for the real world. What they need to be is *smart* about the threats in the world around them. And they need to feel that they can handle these threats intelligently and creatively.

Be open about discussing the dangers in the world with them, in an age-appropriate way. For a younger child, you might focus on things like what they can do if they get separated from Mom. There's no need to frighten a preschooler with the idea that someone could kidnap them. They're not capable of handling that information and couldn't do much to stop it if it did happen. Instead, have them memorize their name, your name and your telephone number. Have them practice dialing it on the phone. Suggest they find a woman ("another mommy") and ask for help if they get lost. Realize that their minds think a little differently, too. Studies have shown that young children don't think of *themselves* as being lost—they think of *mommy* as being lost. So make sure they understand what you mean when you talk about being separated from each other. Encourage them to think of things they could do if that happened. Gently correct ideas and actions that wouldn't be smart. A three-year-old announcing "I'll walk home from the store" might be told, "Well, if you can't find Mommy, Mommy will be looking for you, so it's better to stay close to where you were when you lost Mommy, don't you think? Then I'll know where to look for you."

Older children can have slightly more sophisticated discussions with you about the threats to their safety that might exist. They can also be asked to memorize more detailed information, like your address and the name of the city you live in, and names and phone numbers of grandparents or family friends who could help them if they couldn't reach you right away. Show them a map of the city and talk about various landmarks between your house and places you routinely go. When you drive or walk throughout your city, point out street signs so they know their way around and show them pay phones and convenience stores where they might ask for help if they need it. Ask them to be navigator and direct you as you return home. It's a fun game that teaches them a lot about where they live.

It's important to remember that these threats don't just come from random strangers who might want to hurt them, but can happen when a friend decides to steal something from a store or starts experimenting with drugs or alcohol. All of these various issues fall under the realm of being smart instead of safe. Your children will be exposed to many dangers. If you can teach them some smart moves, they'll be better equipped to handle the threats.

Exercise

How can your kids be smart when feeling threatened? Teach these simple strategies:

- Setting boundaries: If someone they don't know grabs or touches them, they can say, "You're not my mother!" or "You're not my father!" That can draw the attention of bystanders and even scare off an attacker. They can say to a friend, "I don't like it when you call me names when you're mad" or "I don't feel comfortable going to your house when your parents aren't home." By doing so, they're communicating what's important to them and making their own rules about what they want and how they expect others to treat them.

- Saying no: Bureau of Justice statistics show that as many as 50 percent of all attacks are stopped when the defender yells "No!" or something similar. Saying what you want is important. Teach your children to yell "No!" and encourage them to do it if they're afraid or feel threatened.
- Looking for what they can do: Instead of focusing on what they can't do in a self-defense situation, they should look for what they *can* do. If they can't find Mommy, can they find another woman to help? If they can't find a phone, can they pull a fire alarm?

40

Teach appreciation in your family

One of the things traditional martial artists do is express appreciation for each other. They bow to each other, thank each other after they practice together and acknowledge that other people contribute to their success as martial artists. They know that this reduces conflict and makes everyone feel valued.

When families appreciate each other, tensions are reduced, misunderstandings are avoided and the atmosphere tends to be a little calmer. Courtesy, which was discussed earlier (Lesson #18), is an important component of appreciation, but appreciating each other doesn't have to be formal. It's not just about good manners. Maya Angelou quotes her mother as saying, "If you have only one smile in you, give it to the people you love. Don't be surly at home, then go out in the street and start grinning 'Good morning' at total strangers." She has a good point.

A colleague, Rosie Colombraro, says, "This is kind of corny, but every time one member of my family goes somewhere, even if it's to the store, we say 'I love you.' It's something I started doing after my dad left one morning after visiting and kissed me on the cheek and said 'I love you.' He died of a massive heart attack a few hours later."

Having rituals of appreciation like this is meaningful to children. Rosie says, "I never thought my kids paid attention to it until I said good-bye to my adult stepdaughter one day. She started to walk away and then turned and said, 'What, you don't love me anymore?'"

Saying "I love you" whenever anyone goes out the door is a simple way to show the people in your family that you appreciate them. Even if you're a little mad at them, you can bring yourself to say "I love you" and not only does it help smooth over the tension, it reminds you that you do love each other, even if you're having some conflict at the moment.

Exercise

Develop a ritual that shows you appreciate each other. It can be something like Rosie's "I love you" every time someone walks out the door, or it can be an inside joke or a phrase you use. When Jessica was younger, her dad would always say, "Give me five!" when she accomplished something he was proud of. She calls it "clap hands!" I would always use the silly phrase "Awesome, blossom!" to signal the same thing. Now Jessica and I have combined the two and use them whenever we want to express appreciation for each other. One of us will say, "Clap hands!" and the other one says, "Awesome, blossom!" It gives her a big grin and makes me feel like she knows how much I love and appreciate her.

41
Trust your intuition

Beyond the words we use, we communicate with each other via body language and other signals. On a level we don't consciously understand, we often know intuitively when someone is saying something they don't mean, or pretending an emotion they don't feel. We can't pinpoint what exactly gives this information away, but we're aware of it. We get a "funny feeling" or decide we "don't feel good about the situation."

In martial arts training, we try to learn to use our intuition to help keep us safe. We know that, on a subconscious level, we can sometimes sense when someone means us harm. Yet we frequently dismiss our intuition as "silly" or think we're overreacting. And sometimes we are. But as the martial artist learns, it's better to turn around and walk back into the mall if you feel nervous about the five Sumo-wrestler-size men hanging around the parking lot than to brazen it out just to see what happens. You can't measure preventative self-defense—you'll never know when the action you take keeps you safe. But you know that when you don't listen to your intuition, you sometimes find yourself threatened.

I teach people in my self-defense classes to build their

awareness and to learn to listen to their intuition. You "know" more than you think. On an instinctual level, you respond to movements, body language, even scents, of which you are not consciously aware. Trusting these instincts can help you stay safe.

In the same way, building your awareness skills reinforces what your instincts are telling you. If you trust your intuition and build your awareness, you're often able to spot what you instinctively sense to be a threat—the car that's been parked across the street with the driver looking at a map for an hour, the flash of movement as someone tries to get out of your line of vision. Being aware of and engaged in your surroundings helps you trust your intuition.

This works the same way with our children. As writer and mother Dana Anderson-Villamagna says, "What's helped me most was advice from my mom: Trust your own instincts regarding your children. You know them best. If a doctor says your little one's not sick and you sense otherwise, get a second opinion . . . and a third and a fourth, if need be. If advice in The Expert's Book to let them 'cry it out' doesn't feel right when you do it, go and comfort your little one. There are lots of experts out there, and none is as expert as you are on your child."

Because of your awareness of your child, even on a level you may not consciously process, you're more likely to sense when something is truly unusual or out of character for your child. Listen to your inner voice—respect it and trust it.

Build your awareness of your child. Know what is typical for him. Understand what things contribute to problems. For instance, I always had the sense that when I was stressed and overwhelmed, Jessica had more seizures (my mother also noticed this connection). Later, I read studies that linked a child's stress level with increased seizure activity. And if you're a mama, then you know that when Mama's stressed, everyone's stressed. Yet long before I read these studies, I had taken steps to reduce our stress level—and it worked.

Exercise

Trust your instincts. You do know your child better than anyone else—even if it's your first, brand-new baby. If she's always placid and goes right to sleep at night, but is now shrieking and pulling her knees up to her tummy, you can guess that something's not quite right. (Maybe a tummy ache?) Don't disregard what you "know." Yes, sometimes you may be wrong, but that does not mean you should ignore what your instincts are telling you.

- Be willing to throw advice out the window if your heart and your instincts tell you it's not right for your child. One mother was told her son had scored in the retarded range on an intelligence test in grade school. The school wanted to label him a special student and put him in a special education classroom. His mother did not think the label was correct and refused. She never told him the results of the test and always held him to high standards. Some years later, this "retarded" child became a medical doctor.
- Keep track of information that can help you make your case. Jessica has certain symptoms when her shunt fails. Unfortunately, they are almost exactly the same symptoms she has when she's sick with the flu. The one difference I've noticed is that when she has shunt problems, she also complains of headache. So when she seems to

have the flu but also complains of a headache, it's time for a doctor's visit. (I would probably be more relaxed if her shunt hadn't already failed three times.) I bring records with me indicating what her symptoms have been when her shunt has failed previously, and this ensures that the doctors take my concerns seriously— even when it does turn out that Jessica just has the flu.

- Pay attention to the way your children normally behave and notice differences when they're sick or worried about something. One mother noticed that her son chewed his lip only every now and then. Over time, she learned to recognize this as a sign that he had something weighing on his mind that he wanted to talk about but for some reason didn't want to bring up. Knowing this, whenever she saw the signal, she could gently start a conversation with him about what was bothering him. It made a lot of difference in her ability to help him get through some difficult grade school transitions.

42

Protect the beginner

When a beginner starts training in martial arts, she isn't just thrown into the ring with a black belt and told to spar. Instead, she is shown the basic techniques. Then she works with a partner, using little or no contact, moving slowly through the drills. Over time, she is pushed to become faster and stronger and to be comfortable with heavier physical contact. At all levels, but especially at the beginner level, the rules and expectations are set in place to protect her from harm that she may not be capable of protecting herself from.

The same should be true for our children. "Survival of the fittest" may be how evolution works, but it's not how parenting works—at least, it shouldn't be. We're mediators between our child and the outside world. We set the rules and expectations so that we can keep our child free from harm that she may not be capable of protecting herself from. And just as the beginning martial artist grows into the black belt who can handle more challenges, so too do our children grow into adults who no longer need to be protected by us (although if we're lucky, they'll still consult us).

As a parent, it's your job to introduce your child slowly and gradually into the world so that by the time she's an adult, she's able to face the demands and pressures. As author Dorothy Canfield Fisher puts it, "A mother is not a person to lean on but a person to make leaning unnecessary."

This is why it's not unreasonable of you to refuse to let your children watch movies you feel are inappropriate, and why you should set rules about Internet and computer use. It means it's okay for you to refuse to buy thong underwear for your eight-year-old and to restrict reading materials to what is age-appropriate. Does this mean your child won't be exposed to vulgarity and violence? Of course not. But just because they'll be exposed to it elsewhere doesn't mean you have to throw up your hands and think, "Well, everyone else lets their seven-year-olds play Ultimate Extreme Violent Bloodsport IV, so I guess there's no harm if I do."

It's okay to protect the beginner. In fact, it's necessary. And age alone doesn't equate to maturity or ability to handle the outside world. Your five-year-old might be frightened by the (to us) sweet and friendly monsters in *Monsters,*

Inc., while the next-door neighbor kid of the same age loves the movie. That's okay. It's up to you to know that and to act on it. Jessica has always loved every creepy, crawly thing that scuttles into the house and she gets into shoving matches with the dog over who has the privilege of chasing the creatures across the floor. When a field mouse turned up drowned in the toilet, she expressed a clinical interest in it ("Eyeballs are popping out!" she explained to me as she squatted close to the toilet to get a good look while I was hyperventilating by the sink). On the other hand, her cousin absolutely hates anything that doesn't walk upright on two legs. She shrieks in terror over flies and beetles and runs to the nearest adult and launches herself into their arms. That's okay, too. Over time, she'll stop being so scared and won't need to be protected anymore.

By protecting the beginner, you can make sure she develops the best tools to thrive as an adult.

E x e r c i s e

Let other parents know what your rules are for your child. If he's not allowed to watch PG movies, let them know so that they won't screen them when your child is visiting their house (and if they do it anyway, time to re-evaluate whether this is an appropriate house for your child to visit). Don't be embarrassed to ask questions that will ultimately protect your child—including the one that far too few people ask, which is, "Do you keep a gun in this house?" A lot of senseless tragedy could be prevented if more parents kept guns off the premises and if more parents specifically asked this question.

By letting your child know that you set rules to protect him, you're also letting him know that you love him and want him to mature and develop into a happy, healthy adult.

43

Accept criticism to grow

If no one ever gave the martial artist any feedback, she'd never know if she was doing anything right. And if no one ever criticized her—if no one ever told her that she was holding her foot wrong when she kicked, or that the punch in *Dan Gun* form is a high punch—she'd never learn the techniques correctly. And she wouldn't be a very effective martial artist.

And just as we sometimes criticize and correct our children in order for them to grow up to be competent, compassionate adults, as mothers we have to accept criticism to grow ourselves. This can be difficult to do. I know I get very defensive about my mothering skills and I don't particularly care to hear if someone thinks I'm doing something "wrong." On the other hand, if there's a technique or approach I could use with Jessica that would help make our relationship smoother and happier, I know I'd want to hear about it.

So I try to be open to criticism. Not that people approach me and say things like, "Gee, you're a terrible mother, maybe you should take some parenting classes." What they say is something like, "You know, when my daughter went through that stage where she pulled the dog's tail no matter how often I told her not to, I tried this approach. . . ." And if I'm open to it and don't feel defensive about it, I can try the idea and it might, indeed, work for me.

But more important, I try to listen to the criticism that Jessica gives me. I don't mean the "You're so mean 'cause

you won't let me buy all the stickers at Hobby Lobby" criticism. I mean the more subtle signs and signals that she
gives out. For example, during a period when I was overwhelmed with work, my sitters were being unreliable, my ex
had bailed on taking Jessica for a couple of weekends in a
row, the dogs were peeing on the carpet instead of on the
grass and Jessica had suddenly become very demanding of
my attention, she would ask me a question and then cover
her ears because the likelihood that I was going to yell was
apparently pretty high. (Okay, that's not such a subtle sign.)
And yes, I felt like an enormous jerk, but you're not a
mother if you haven't had the opportunity to feel pretty
small sometimes.

Obviously Jessica's criticism made me grow as a mother.
It made me realize that no matter how many pressures I had
in other areas of my life, I had to be calmer and more patient
when I was dealing with Jessica. And I'm glad to report that
I did accomplish this, and she doesn't have to cover her ears
when she asks me a question these days.

E x e r c i s e

What subtle and not-so-subtle criticisms are you getting from
those around you? Are they valid? Sometimes, of course, you'll be
criticized for doing exactly what a mother should do, so you don't
need to make any changes. But other times paying attention to criticism will help you grow as a mother.

44
Your child can do more
than you believe possible

One of the most wonderful experiences in martial arts comes when you launch your forty-year-old body into the air and execute a jump spinning wheel kick. (It feels good no matter what age you are.) No one thought you could do it—least of all, you. But there you are, jumping and spinning and striking. If you can do that, you can do anything.

Just as we shortchange ourselves all the time by not giving ourselves credit for what we can accomplish, sometimes we shortchange our children as well. Often this is because we want to protect them (see Lesson #42). While it's a good goal to protect your children from dangerous and inappropriate influences, it's also important not to hold your children back, but to let them discover that they can do a lot more than they believed possible.

Having high standards for children makes them feel good about themselves. Real self-esteem comes from being able to do things, solve problems, work through difficulties on your own. And children know this. That's why they want to spread their wings and fly while we're busy running around with mattresses to cushion their fall.

But our children can do more than we think. We should encourage them to do as much as possible. When we let them—encourage them—to do the equivalent of the jump spinning wheel kick, it gives them a strong sense that they're capable and competent, and that they can do anything they set their minds to. What a terrific belief to have!

Because I believe all members of the family should contribute to the family (even the dogs entertain, protect and love us), I knew Jessica needed to be doing at least one significant chore around the house. So I proposed that she help me do the dishes by gathering the dirty plates and cups from the table and putting away the clean silverware and cookie sheets. This proved to be something she enjoyed doing and she frequently announced to me that she was a "big help!" And she was.

Imagine my surprise and delight when one day after finishing a phone call in my office, I came into the kitchen to see my six-year-old daughter putting away the last dish from a load we'd just washed that morning. Despite being cognitively and visually impaired, she'd emptied the dishwasher and put all the dishes away by herself. I didn't realize she could do that. It just never occurred to me.

Now I let her empty the dishwasher every day. (I take out the sharp knives first.) To reach the high shelves, she carries the dishes to the counter beneath the appropriate cabinet, carries her stepstool and positions it on the floor next to the counter, then climbs up the step stool and puts the dishes away. And in the right places every time—because she watched me and paid attention. Imagine how competent that makes her feel. I know many six-year-olds without Jessica's challenges and I don't know one who does this by herself, although obviously they're capable of doing so. Our children can do more than we believe. We should encourage them to try.

Take stock of what you expect from your children and what you let them do. They can probably do more than you allow. At least entertain the notion that this could be true. I know plenty of kids who had never done a load of laundry when they moved out or went to college. Ridiculous. A ten- or twelve-year-old is perfectly capable of learning how to do this. Not being dependent on someone else to provide for them makes children feel more powerful in their lives. Let them spread their wings—and instead of running around with mattresses, have faith that they can do it.

45

The Way is different for every mother

Although I think practicing the martial arts is a terrific way to spend your life, not everyone is meant to be a martial artist. And of the people who are meant to be martial artists, not all of them are meant to be *Hapkidoin* or *Karateka* (practioners of Hapkido or Karate). The Way is different for everyone. For some people, it's smashing concrete blocks with your hands; for others, it's running the Boston Marathon.

Just because other mothers act a certain way or do certain things doesn't mean that you need to. When I first became a mother, I tried to act like other mothers—so instead of being a mother, finding my own place and my own way of doing things, I was sort of playing one on TV (only I wasn't on TV). Since other mothers wore their hair short because it was easier with a baby, I cut my hair. I instantly regretted it, which I would have been able to guess if I hadn't been so convinced I needed to be like other mothers. That's how silly I was. Why didn't I find out first if having long hair worked for me or not?

Gradually, I lightened up a bit. Just because other parents gave their children only gluten-free cereal snacks did not mean I couldn't get away with a Cheerio now and then, or even—gasp!—a McDonald's French fry. I became bolder. I paid a sitter to take Jessica for walks because I thought it would do her good but I had work to do. When I got divorced, the duplex I moved into was small and my bedroom didn't have room for all of my office equipment *and* my bed so I put the bed in the living room, not far from the heavy bag.

When Jessica expressed interest in punching and kicking the heavy bag, I gave her a child-size one for her birthday. My martial arts instructor gave me a set of sparring gloves for her. (For Christmas, an aunt gave her dress-up clothes and when Jessica saw the lovely pink satin elbow-length evening gloves, she held them up curiously and I said, "Those are gloves," and her eyes lit up and she said, "Hit the bag, Mama! Hit the bag!")

In other words, I don't think the other mothers on the block are exactly like me. But that's okay, because I bet they have their own way of mothering.

Exercise

Find your own way. You know what's important to you as a mother, and as a person. It's good for children to have mothers who are real people with intense interests, likes and dislikes of their own. (As Ariel Gore says, "Children need interesting mothers.") Just because the other mothers in the group or on the block do it doesn't mean you have to, and just because they don't doesn't mean you shouldn't. The Way is different for everyone.

46
Model well-rounded skills

Each different martial arts style focuses on teaching different types of skills. In Jujitsu, grappling techniques are important; in Karate, the emphasis is on striking techniques. In Tae Kwon Do, my main style, the focus is on kicks. So when I spar opponents, they expect me to use kicks. That's why I developed an arsenal of punching techniques and learned how to use them against all kinds of opponents. The punches are unexpected in a Tae Kwon Do practitioner. Sometimes they're exactly why I win the match.

As a matter of fact, learning martial arts was an unexpected skill in the first place! No one who knew me before I began studying Tae Kwon Do would ever have expected it from me. But by doing the unexpected, I was able to learn and grow as a person, develop a new career and create a life I love.

As a parent, it's good to learn and use different skills. Often all our children see us do is go to work (they don't know much about our work), then come home, eat a meal, maybe watch television or read a book. On weekends, everyone is busy running around to soccer games and getting groceries. Your children may never see the skills that you've developed in your life.

By taking the time to show your children the many different things you know but rarely show off, you can introduce your children to a world of opportunities. I remember when my mother, who loved to draw but rarely did it because raising six kids doesn't leave a lot of time for leisurely sketching under the oak tree, dug out her old chalks and charcoal and showed me how to sketch. I was wretched at it but became very interested in art (even ended up writing about art and art history early in my career).

Your children can participate or do as I did when my dad fixed the car, which was to hang over his shoulder asking, "Whatcha doin' now?" (Hey, I learned to gap spark plugs. Unfortunately it's not a skill that has proven to have much value for me, but considering how clearly I remember those visits to the garage, a lot of useful interaction was going on.)

The skills you show and share with your children don't have to be complex or sophisticated. For example, although mothers in general don't tend to roughhouse with their children (that's a dad thing), one of my joys in life is slinging Jessica over my shoulder and carrying her from room to room like "Mama's sack of potatoes." She gets deposited, breathless and giggling, on her bed. I remember very clearly my father doing the same thing for me. Carrying a little kid around like a sack of potatoes doesn't have to be a dad thing, and Jessica enjoys the unexpected skill Mama displays.

Exercise

You can be a good role model by showing your kids that people can have many interests and abilities. Maybe this is the year that you plant a garden for the first time since you had kids. Your children can help you plan the garden, pick out the seeds, plant them (don't expect them to stick with the weeding, though). Showing well-rounded skills doesn't have to take a lot of time—in other words, you don't have to make cabinets in your spare time to impress your children. You can dig your old poetry journal out of the closet and share it with your child. That might inspire her to start her own. Or show your kids how to throw a pot, then leave them to the clay. Take a moment to think about all the things you know how to do but don't do anymore because you don't have time, have stopped being interested or started paying someone to do it instead. Find a way to share those skills with your children. You can spark their love of learning and create some wonderful parent-child times.

47
Use the teachable moment

When you spar an opponent and you're trying to score a point, you focus on the openings—you focus on the targets where you can score a point. You don't focus on the fact that your opponent has a good guard and that you don't know how you're going to get past it. You focus on what you can do, not what you can't. You look for the opportunities and sometimes you create the opportunities.

For mothers, we might call this "finding the teachable moments." Instead of sitting down and lecturing your children about scientific discoveries, let them take the lead. Jessica once went looking for the moon and couldn't find it (she blamed the dogs for eating the moon, which made logical sense seeing as they eat everything else that gets left out). That was a perfect teachable moment for me to talk to her about what the moon and the stars are, and how the moon rises and sets just like the sun. Now imagine me sitting her down at the table one Monday morning and beginning a lecture out of the blue: "Jessica, you know how you see the moon in the sky at night? The moon is a satellite. . . ." Right.

When our dog Dakota howls at Jessica, that's an opportunity for me to remind her that we're gentle with animals, and we wouldn't want them pulling our hair. It's more meaningful than an abstract conversation about compassion would be. When I'm with Jessica, I try to focus on those openings so we can learn and grow together.

Exercise

While it's wise to let your kids take the lead—there will almost always be opportunities for you to communicate important concepts if you focus on the moments they bring to you—sometimes you do need to take the initiative. When my mother was pregnant with my little sister, I expressed no interest in how babies were made, but my mother decided it was time I learned and so she took the opportunity for a sex education session. I was bored to tears but I understood how my little sister came about, and that was the main thing my mother wished to communicate. The opening she saw was her pregnancy, and even though I didn't initiate the conversation, she was still able to take the opportunity to teach me something important.

Find the openings and you'll have an engaged, interested student rather than one who is distracted and doesn't pay attention.

48

Find your passion

Martial arts is my passion—Tae Kwon Do in particular. I've trained in other styles, and I've even tried other sports, like basketball and skiing, but my personal passion is Tae Kwon Do. Nothing compares to how I feel about stepping into the training hall and working out. Oh, I'll lift weights because it's good for me, and I'll go hiking with friends if I have to, but my athletic passion is martial arts. So I focus on my passion. I put a heavy bag in my living room, I keep bag gloves on top of the bookshelf, I keep books about martial arts on hand so I can double-check how that form is done when I'm training on my own. I sign up for seminars and belong to martial arts discussion groups. I do everything I can to feed my passion.

As a mother, I try to find my passion, too. I try to find the one thing about motherhood that makes it all worthwhile to me. That's what I focus on when things get a little dicey. With Jessica, it's her giggle. She has the greatest giggle in the world, and hearing it makes me happy I'm her mother. So when she's being otherwise impossible, or when she's sick and I'm tired and worried, I think about what I love about motherhood. And I love hearing Jessica giggle. My sister Beth says the thing she focuses on is Alexis's devilish grin. Whenever she thinks about that grin, she gets all mushy inside and it makes her feel more loving and patient toward Alexis, even if Alexis happens to be screaming in her ear. My niece Elizabeth says it's her daughter Hailey's practice of pulling her shirt up to look at her stomach when she's full.

Finding your passion as a mother also means doing what you can to keep the flames burning bright—instead of burning out. This might include things like being sure to get enough time for yourself. Perhaps it includes talking over parenting goals with your friends, brainstorming solutions to work-life balance issues with your goal buddy, sharing kid stories with anyone who'll hold still long enough to listen. When your passion for mothering needs to be rekindled, maybe all you need to do is look over a scrapbook or journal you keep to remind you of why you treasure your children so much.

If you walk into my office, you don't see a framed picture of Jessica, you see twenty of them. I surround myself with reminders of my passion so that I can focus on the good stuff, the reasons I love having Jessica. Now if I could just find a foolproof way to get her to giggle, I'd be set for life.

Exercise

Sometimes in our hectic days, we forget what we love about being mothers and when we lose sight of that, it's easy get a bit overwhelmed and feel burned out. So find your passion—the one thing about motherhood that makes everything else disappear—and write it down, like an affirmation. Post it above your computer or on your mirror. Take a look at it when things get hard. Focus on what makes motherhood meaningful to you. Find the passion and make it the focus of your positive thoughts.

49
Heart is more important than talent

I have a dear friend who shall remain nameless since I'm about to point out that she's not the most competent woman in the world. She doesn't cook or sew or clean house or hold down a job, and the thought of doing something like assembling a bookshelf from pieces in a carton is enough to send her into a tailspin. She's a little ditzy. Okay, a lot ditzy. Her socks never match. Still, she's cheerful and a lot of fun—and she managed to raise an incredibly talented, creative daughter who was running her own business by the age of eighteen. What matters is that my friend loves her daughter and tries to do the best she can. I'd say she succeeded. In mothering, as in many things, having heart is far more important than having talent.

I first discovered this when I began training in martial arts. I would see an incredibly athletic and talented martial artist who could do the most complicated throws and the most spectacular spinning kicks after being shown once. And I would see the student who, try as she might, would fall on her butt every time she did a flying side kick. You'd think the talented ones would be the students who earned their black belts. Much of the time you'd be wrong. Achieving success in martial arts has more to do with having heart—passion, commitment, focus, discipline, perseverance—than it does raw talent. You can have lots of talent but if you don't have passion and commitment, you won't succeed as a black belt.

For mothers, having heart—love for your child, the desire to give your child the best life possible—is much more important than any abstract idea like talent. I know some first-time mothers who have a glowing pregnancy, pop out their babies, sling 'em on the breast and get back to work inside of a month, but for the rest of us mere mortals, the reality that we are something less than ideal mothers must be faced. It's also not very important. As with anything you learn, you go through trial and error and you make mistakes. Unfortunately, the tasks keep changing just as you master them. You figure out how to get a diaper changed on a squirming newborn in twelve seconds flat only to be faced with a nine-month-old who rolls over as soon as the diaper comes off and scoots as fast as she can in the opposite direction. You finally wean your baby but now have to figure out how to teach her to use a spoon and a fork without splattering all four walls and the ceiling with spaghetti sauce. You finally teach the kid how to look both ways when he crosses the street and now he wants to learn to ride a bike.

So whenever you feel a little down on yourself for not measuring up to some abstract ideal, remember that heart is more important than talent.

Exercise

If you sometimes feel you're not doing a good job as a mother, ask yourself these simple questions: Do I love my child? Am I doing the best I can to raise her in the way I think is right?

That's all you need to know.

50
Observe without judging

When you're with other parents and their children, you can observe them from a position of either "I don't do it that way so it must be wrong," or you can watch without judging, see how the technique works, ask questions about it (if appropriate) and then try it yourself to see if it might work for you.

The ability to observe without judging helps you consider new ways of doing things and new approaches to old problems. After a martial artist has trained in an art for a number of years—enough to understand the system and to have made strides toward mastering the techniques—commonly she'll start to explore other martial arts, just to see what else is out there and what techniques and ideas she might pick up to improve her own skills and abilities.

Either she can see another martial arts technique and think, "That's not the way we do it! That's wrong and stupid and ineffective," or she can watch without judging. She can see how the practitioner does the technique. She can ask what its purpose is. She can try it herself to see if it might be effective for her. But she must first observe without judging and making comparisons.

When I met my friend Julie for the first time, she was feeding her daughter Chloe, then about eleven months old, big chunks of cantaloupe and seedless watermelon. At first I was surprised because I was still feeding nine-month-old Jessica little itty-bitty pieces of food cut up so small you could hardly see them on the plate. But instead of judging ("Chloe could choke on those big pieces of fruit!") I watched Chloe gobble the fruit down and I realized that Jessica was probably capable of graduating to chewable food as well—so I tried it and found I was right. It saved a lot of work for me and made Jessica feel competent and grown-up.

One mother I know used to extol the virtues of a Montessori education to everyone within reach. And her daughter certainly seemed amazingly proficient and advanced. She was reading young-adult novels when she was seven years old, could do multiplication and long division at the same age and also enjoyed playing various musical instruments. Instead of thinking, "Oh, that's much too expensive," or deciding that it would be harmful to a child not to have a typical public school education, one of her friends looked into the option for her own daughter and realized that it was the ideal setting and educational philosophy for their family. She enrolled her daughter and was delighted to have discovered the option—which she doubts she would have even considered if she hadn't observed her friend's experience with the system.

If you're open to what other parents are doing and try it for yourself when appropriate, you can expand your horizons with your child. You can go beyond what you yourself know personally and learn from others.

E x e r c i s e

Practice the technique of observing without judging. At first it doesn't have to be another parent. It could be anyone doing anything. It could be a salesclerk waiting on a customer. Instead of thinking, "I would do it better and be much more competent," simply watch the interaction, see how it works, ask yourself if there's something you might learn from it. Once you've gotten into the habit, you can apply the same observational skills to afternoons at the playground while watching other parents interact with their children.

51
Know yourself

I love to spar. I enjoy it more than any other aspect of training. I know this about myself. I realize that I have to work on other parts of my training, like doing forms and working on my conditioning, but I also know that I should play to my strengths. I focus my time and energy on sparring techniques. Yes, I practice forms, because they're part of the martial arts, but I know myself, and I know what interests me is sparring, so I let myself spar.

As a mother, I've found it's important for me to know myself and use my strengths. For example, I love having Jessica as a companion, so I bring her with me whenever I travel, even on business. She's learned to fly, eat at nice restaurants and she has visited the Smithsonian and the Metropolitan Museum of Art. I'm a voracious book reader, so I buy her more books than is strictly necessary. We read them together every night. I love doing art projects—get out the crayons and sequins and glue and I'm good to go. I like having her help me do household chores. She learns a lot and enjoys it.

But as for playing board games and card games, which I know are good for teaching turn taking and counting and other excellent skills? Forget about it. I know these are good things for a kid to do, so when I hire someone to watch her,

I make sure they understand that part of the deal is playing Chutes and Ladders all afternoon. Imagine how nice it is for everyone when the sitter who enjoys playing board games gets to do it with Jessica, who also loves them.

A long time ago, I would have tried to change myself, but you know what? It's okay that I don't like to play board games. I know she gets lots of good experiences with me doing other things. I don't have to be the one to teach her everything. I also know that she could tell that I don't like to play these games, and she thought it meant I didn't like to play with her. And I am not willing to hurt her that way.

The truth is, we all have strengths and it's smart to use them. Instead of pretending our weaknesses don't exist, let's admit them, find someone to take over and move along.

Exercise

You don't have to do every single thing with your children that The Experts tell you that you must. If you'd rather everyone stay out of your kitchen when you're cooking dinner, that's okay. Maybe Dad or Grandma can teach the fine art of baking muffins. Focus on what you love to do with your children. Do that. You'll have to do some of the other stuff, like wash their hair and supervise their tooth brushing, but if you focus on your strengths, your children will respond to the joy you have when you're doing that with them. They'll notice if you really dislike doing certain things. Instead of letting them take it personally—they'll think it has something to do with them—delegate the disliked activity to someone else who enjoys it. You play to your strengths.

52
Accept hard challenges

As a mother, you'll have the occasional hard challenge—and none of the challenges will be your choice. You didn't sign up for your toddler breaking her arm or your grade-schooler failing his classes or your teenage son getting turned on to drugs or your young daughter turning up pregnant. I certainly didn't sign up for a child with a rare genetic disorder. But it's important to accept the challenges of motherhood instead of trying to deny them or get away from them or pretend they don't exist. If you can accept, then you can learn how to handle the challenges. If you pretend that they can't happen and try to ignore them when they do happen, you'll make a difficult problem infinitely worse.

Martial artists engage in hard training occasionally. A typical training session is not considered hard training—it's considered a typical training session. But now and then the instructor will put together a really difficult program, or the martial artist will sign up for a hard training camp. The idea is to raise your expectations of yourself. When you're challenged, you can find reserves of strength you didn't know you had. If you avoid the hard training, you'll never know if you can do it.

So look on those hard challenges as opportunities to grow and become stronger. When your two-year-old defies every word you say, if you simply accept that this is a stage you'll have to be patient through, you'll survive with fewer ruffled edges than if you try too hard to solve the problem.

The problem is that your child is two, and two-year-olds defy their parents. It will pass. Writer, social psychologist and mother Carin Rubenstein writes, "For parents, the terrible twos are a psychological preview of puberty. At the age of two or three, children eat only bananas and refuse to get a haircut. Ten years later, they eat only bananas and refuse to get a haircut." At least having gotten through the terrible twos will prepare you for adolescence! When your five-year-old doesn't want to get up and go to kindergarten and every morning is a battle, you can accept the challenge and deal with it. Maybe you can do some creative problem-solving (send him to the afternoon kindergarten session, give him something fun to do first thing in the morning before he goes off to school). Maybe you just keep persisting—keep getting him up and making him get ready.

It's important not to ignore the hard challenges, somehow hoping they'll go away. A friend of mine once agonized about bringing her preschool daughter to the ophthalmologist even though she knew her child squinted a lot, seemed to have difficulty focusing and complained of headaches. "I don't want her to have to wear glasses," she said. Certainly any of us can sympathize. But of course it's not fair to the child to ignore the problem.

By being willing to accept the hard challenges, you grow stronger as a mother. You even learn to handle the challenges so they don't seem so hard. The first time I had to explain Jessica's problem to a friend was hard. Experience has made it much easier. You'll find the same happens in your life, too.

Expect that you will have hard challenges as a mother and that you won't always be prepared for what they will be. Try to educate yourself as much as possible about typical challenges experienced at your children's ages. You may still be caught by surprise, but you'll also be more likely to be prepared and able to handle the challenges.

53

Obstacles are opportunities

Martial artists develop the mind-set that they can rise to any challenge. If they have to break boards for a test, why, then, they'll break boards. If they have to spar three opponents at once, why, then, that's what they'll do. These obstacles are an opportunity for the martial artist to develop skill, gain self-confidence and demonstrate her abilities. The obstacles are an opportunity for her to prove herself—a chance for her to notch another successful outcome on her belt.

Turning obstacles into opportunities works for mothers, too. When you see an obstacle, it doesn't have to be a mountain that blocks your way. It can be a little hill that you scoot around. If your little one has chicken pox and to stay home from work you have to take a vacation day that you would much rather have spent lazing on the beach, take the opportunity to do something you haven't done in a while— bake some cookies or read a trashy novel (of course, realizing that your sick kid will be forced to interrupt you if you appear to be having too much fun).

One of my friends remembers an afternoon when she somehow irritated her child so much that he wouldn't speak to her for the rest of the day—he would let only his father feed him and play with him. Instead of trying to cajole him into a good mood, she took a bath and gave herself a facial. Next morning, everything was fine again.

When you have an argument with your child—whether it's over bedtime, the homework that didn't get done, the crayons that mysteriously left marks all over the walls—you can feel terrible about it, or you can think of it as an opportunity to show your child how to compromise and negotiate. If that's not in the works, you can show empathy and explain that you understand his feelings and hope he understands yours. And if you're in the wrong, you can apologize, and show him the power of saying "I'm sorry."

E x e r c i s e

See the opportunity, not the obstacle. When I got divorced, I knew Jessica couldn't be in day care—we had tried it before, unsuccessfully. But I had had some success as a freelance writer, so I took this as an opportunity to become a full-time freelancer, taking care of Jessica during the day and working nights and weekends. Instead of having to go to a boring job as a publicist or an editor, I get to have it all: a job I love and the chance to stay home and raise Jessica. If I had seen only the obstacle—how can I keep a job without Jessica being in day care?—I might not have recognized the opportunity. I might have focused on the wrong sorts of solutions, such as trying to get friends to watch her or hiring a nanny. Instead, by seeing this

as an opportunity to follow a dream—become a freelance writer—
I made that dream a reality.

Finding ways to turn obstacles into opportunities can be a creative pastime for a mother. Private school too expensive? Start your
own charter school. Fund-raising for the local Scout group pretty
dismal? Become the Scout leader yourself and take charge. Local
school board banning books from the school library? Run for office. Don't focus on the obstacle. Focus on what you can do to get
around it.

54

Give your strongest effort
with every try

As parents, we're certainly committed to being patient and
compassionate with our children. But we also know that the
other demands in our lives affect our abilities to be effective
parents. The commitment to give your strongest effort with
every try means that as a parent you won't look for excuses
for less than stellar behavior. In other words, your commitment is to be consistent and effective and loving with your
children in all circumstances—in public and private, when
you're rested and when you're overtired. Expect the very
best from yourself.

The importance of this principle is demonstrated to me
every time I teach. Some martial arts students give their best
effort when the teacher is looking or when they're being
tested for promotion. But when the teacher's back is turned,

the student's technique becomes sloppy and lazy. Unfortunately, this means that she's not practicing good technique all of the time—and it shows. You can't master the techniques if you think it's okay to be sloppy when no one is watching. These students aren't fooling anyone but themselves. Maybe not even themselves. But still, I see it all the time. I wonder what they hope to gain from the practice. What could they possibly get from only occasionally trying hard?

In mothering, the important thing is to know when it will be difficult to give your strongest effort. I know that when I have deadlines looming, I'm likely to be more short-tempered with Jessica. So, knowing this, I try to prepare for it. I try to balance my workload so that by working steadily I accomplish what needs to be done and so that I'm not always rushing around trying to finish things at the last minute. And when I do have a crunch, I remind myself that my deadlines have nothing to do with Jessica and I'm going to have to count to ten a little more often just to stay on an even keel with her.

But just as the martial artist sometimes gets too fatigued to continue training, so too might you experience times when under the circumstances you can't parent as effectively as you'd like—you can't give your strongest effort with every try. The martial artist knows that if she keeps working when she's reached the point of complete fatigue, she'll just be practicing sloppy techniques. And she doesn't want to practice sloppy techniques. She doesn't want to train her body that way—she wants to train her body with the most perfect techniques she can. So when, as a mother, you reach the point of complete fatigue and you know you simply can't continue to give your strongest effort with every try, call in the reinforcements.

Recognize those times when you've reached your saturation point. Take a break. Hire a sitter. Get out of the house; ask the grandparents to take the kids overnight. After rest, you'll be back to giving your best effort with every try.

Exercise

Learn to recognize the symptoms of overload. (Like overtraining, this will lead to setbacks.) I can tell that when I start saying, "What?" in a less-than-pleasant tone of voice when Jessica wants my attention, I need to regroup—and maybe stop trying to do five things at once and instead give her my full attention—or arrange for a break for me. I also keep a mental list of things I can do to regroup—take a shower (some days I am squeaky clean), watch a video with Jess, watch a movie (at a real theater) without her. Get a full eight hours of sleep—even if I have work to do. Meditate. Stretch. You can find some similar tricks that will work for you.

55

Nurture yourself

Even though martial artists push themselves to perform at high levels—to train hard and to dig deep—they also know they need to take care of themselves if they hope to achieve their martial arts goals. They know that being a martial artist is not a sprint—they don't just work hard, reach their goal and then stop. They know that they have to be able to keep training for the rest of their lives. To do that, they need to have balance in their lives. They need to allow themselves rest to balance the exertion. They try to eat right to nourish their bodies, so they can continue to perform. They try to eliminate addictions (like smoking) from their lives, because they know these addictions negatively affect their ability to perform. When they have an injury, they let it heal. They don't want to permanently damage themselves.

Mothers also need to nurture themselves. Psychologist Rick Hanson, the co-author of *Mother Nurture,* says, "A vital piece of mother's wisdom is to take care of yourself so you can take care of your family."

Rick offers some simple, low-cost ways to de-stress:

- Make sure you're getting three healthy meals a day.
- Exercise several times a week.
- Take time for yourself.
- Create a personal practice for your inner being, such as doing a craft or dancing.
- Spend time with supportive friends each week.
- Address significant medical, personal or family issues.

On a moment-to-moment basis, take a deep breath, brew a cup of tea, wash your face, sit in the sun, stretch, pet a dog (or a cat). I'm partial to dog therapy myself and know that a few minutes of petting my Malamute Dakota will give me a feeling of peace and serenity. And it doesn't hurt to teach your children these strategies as well—they'll come in handy. Jessica knows that burying her face in Dakota's fur when she feels a little overwhelmed feels good and helps her calm down. She knows the importance of sitting in the sun and going for a walk when times get a little tough.

Give yourself permission to nurture yourself. As mothers, we tend to look after everyone else first before tending to ourselves. But by making yourself a priority, you can remain happy and healthy—and ready to tackle the challenges of parenting. Dorothy DeBolt, who has six children of her own and adopted fourteen more, says, "Of course I don't always enjoy being a mother. At those times, my husband and I hole up somewhere in the wine country, eat, drink, make mad love and pretend we were born sterile and raise poodles." Sounds good to me.

56
Trust yourself

Mothers need to trust themselves in order to take charge and raise their children without a lot of self-doubt and second-guessing. As psychiatrist Elaine Heffner says, "Staying in charge as a mother means exercising one's own judgment about what is best for one's child. It means, at times, disregarding the advice of experts. It means trusting one's own point of view. Most of all, it means developing the ability to tolerate both the internal anxiety and the external hostility that are generated when one tries to stay in charge." In other words, trust yourself and be confident in yourself despite the nagging little doubts you might have and those dear "friends" of yours who say, "Are you *sure* that's the right thing to do?"

Sometimes it can be difficult to trust yourself, especially when you've made a mistake. When I was a brown belt in Tae Kwon Do, I injured someone in a training accident. I felt awful—an incompetent, terrible martial artist with no self-control. My black-belt test was coming up and I was so afraid of hurting someone, I knew I would not do well on it. (It's hard to show your confident, fearless side when you're worried about hurting someone.) My friends worked with me, pushing me to go harder and to trust myself. Over time, I learned that I had good control, that I could spar well and that I wouldn't be hurting people indiscriminately if left to my own devices. With their help, I began to rebuild my trust in myself, and I've never had it shaken like that again.

So when, as a mother, I have doubts about my ability to cope with a problem or wonder if I'm overreacting to an event, I remember my martial arts experience and realize that I need to trust myself.

Carol Stambaugh, a social worker and the mother of a two-year-old, says, "The best advice came from a friend when Kaeden [Carol's daughter] was about two weeks old. I was freaking out. My friend looked me straight in the eye and said, 'There is no right or wrong way to do things. The right way is the way that works for you.'" Carol says, "I remember that so clearly because we were furiously reading every book we could find on baby sleep patterns and do you let them cry it out, do you stick to a schedule? Every book said something different." Carol learned to stop worrying about the "right" way and the "wrong" way and to instead trust herself as a competent, effective, loving parent. And she feels calmer and more in control because of it.

Toss the parenting books (not this one!). Glean what you can but realize that you will find the techniques that work for you. The Expert doesn't know your situation, your challenges, your concerns, your worldview, your hopes or your relationship with your child.

And don't forget to honor yourself when you've handled a milestone effectively. Consciously remembering and acknowledging what you've done as a parent helps reinforce the message that you can be trusted with the care of this other delightful living creature. You celebrate your baby's first step; why not celebrate the first time your baby had a tantrum and you handled it just fine?

57

Your mothering strength can be a weakness

Our strengths as mothers can sometimes backfire. We are strong, we can weather tough times, we can stay up with a colicky baby and still give a brilliant presentation the next day at work. Those are strengths, all good. But sometimes they can backfire.

I often look at it this way. One of my strengths in sparring is using hand techniques. Opponents are expecting kicks, and so they're surprised when I do so many punches. But that strength can also be a weakness. If I punch, I have to be closer to my opponent than if I kick, and a good opponent will keep me from being able to punch by using kicks to keep me away.

As mothers we may not realize that our strengths can be a weakness. They may mean we're not give ourselves the care we need. And we may make ourselves the focus of our child's life—all their needs must be met by us—which is challenging and unrealistic. Your child will never have another relationship where one person can meet all his needs. Why assume you must just because you're the mommy?

I fell into this trap a lot, particularly after Jessica's father and I divorced. I could do it all. I could homeschool her and raise her and work full-time as a freelance writer. I could teach her martial arts and math and dog care. I was strong and capable, and very, very tired.

Eventually, Jessica's speech therapist convinced me to add a special tutor to her life. So I did, a wonderful young woman who came over once or twice a week and took Jessica to the park and worked on phonics with her. Then I brought a yoga teacher in to help make sure Jessica got the physical exercise she needed. I no longer had to be in charge of everything—and that was good. Jessica loves these teachers and their presence helps make me a more effective mother. So my strength—being there for Jessica, making her the center of my world—also represented a weak spot. By taking action, I made sure that I didn't bankrupt my energy, and that I didn't burn out with the demands on me.

Suppose one of your mothering strengths is your efficiency. You can dress two toddlers and a preschooler, feed them breakfast and have them playing in the park by 8 a.m. You can keep the house spic-and-span, balance the checkbook, creatively cut costs and create delectable meals three times a day seven days a week. Definitely a strength. But in some ways, it can be a weakness. Perhaps it prevents your spouse from having a more important role in child and home care. Maybe it would be a good thing (for everyone) if he were more involved. So now and then maybe you should burn the roast and order pizza.

One of my friends is incredibly competent. Certainly a good thing. She can fix a plugged sink, build a bookcase, make gorgeous jewelry to give as gifts (of course with home-made cards). But when her little ones want to help, she politely declines because they'll just make a mess. But helping out, exploring the world, seeing what happens when you use a hammer instead of a screwdriver to put in a screw, spilling the sequins all over the floor and gluing the cat's tail to the carpet—these are all things children learn from. (The cat learns, too.)

Recognize that there may be drawbacks to your strengths. It's okay to be a little inefficient, slightly incompetent and occasionally downright temperamental.

Exercise

What are your strengths? Are you really hands-on? Could that be a weakness—could you be *too* hands-on? Is your strength that you sit back and let your child grow? Are you too hands-off? Could more balance help you as a parent while at the same time benefiting your child?

Often knowing we have certain strengths blinds us to the trade-offs that go along with them. And if we don't give ourselves the care we need, we can easily burn out, become depressed (or even just blue) and discover that we're not living life to the fullest. But by making sure our strength is really a strength, and getting the support we need, we can keep going for as long as necessary.

58
Act instead of hoping

As mothers, we know it's smarter to act than it is to hope that everything will be fine. When you're pregnant, you go to prenatal checkups. You don't just hope you'll have a healthy baby and labor and delivery will go fine. When your child has a mysterious rash, you take her to the doctor to find out what it is.

Just as a martial artist knows that if she wants to master a new technique, she'll have to work to learn it, understand it and perform it, a mother recognizes that if she wants some help around the house, it isn't going to magically appear. The martial artist doesn't just see someone do the new technique and think, "Gee, I wish I could do that," and somehow expect miracles. She knows that there's nothing magic about how she's going to learn that new technique. She's not going to read about it and pick it up by mental telepathy or osmosis. She's going to practice it over and over. She's going to invest physical effort in mastering the technique. She's going to fall down, and she's going to get sore muscles, but she's going to do the work.

We mothers recognize that we have to do the work. But the fact is, much of a mother's life requires the ability to wait and see. If her child isn't walking by age twelve months, her pediatrician will probably say, "Let's wait and see." And there's nothing wrong with that. There's nothing wrong with waiting and seeing (and very probably hoping at the same time), if that's the appropriate choice to take, if there's no better action that should be pursued.

Very often, though, we can—and need to—take action instead of hoping everything will be all right. When your one-year-old doesn't start walking, you *do* take her to the pediatrician even though the pediatrician may say, "Let's wait and see." Because it might be that some special treatment is needed. If you had relied on hope, you might have missed the opportunity to solve the problem.

When your seven-year-old fails math one semester, you don't hope he'll do better next year. You take action. Pinpointing the problem, working with the teacher, hiring a tutor, rewarding study. And by doing so, you teach him that *he* needs to act instead of hoping. If he intends to pass his math class, he's going to have to do more than hope he'll score a good grade on the final. He has to study and prepare and memorize the formulas.

By acting instead of hoping, we do what we can to ensure that we meet our goals and that we're caring for our children as best we can.

Exercise

Determine what actions you can take to solve a problem. We often rely on hope when we don't really want to face the problem, or when we're undecided about what to do, or when we don't want to think about what needs to be done because it's probably going to be hard or require money or skills that we don't have.

So instead of trusting ourselves to solve the problem, we hope it goes away.

Instead, identify what the problem is—write it down. Your infant vomits after every meal. Your toddler seems to have an excessive number of tantrums. Your potty-trained kid has started wetting the bed at night. Then—maybe with a friend or your partner—brainstorm the actions you can take, in the order you should take them. The vomiting baby needs to see the doctor to rule out a serious health problem. If all tests are negative, maybe changing the baby's diet will help. Your tantruming toddler might be helped if you could figure out triggers. Your first step may be to keep a journal, jotting down when and where and why he seems to have tantrums. You may find that he isn't having as many as you think he is. You may find that a certain pattern occurs. Your next step might be to educate yourself on different approaches to handling tantrums and deciding on which approach to try first. Your bed-wetting child should be brought to the doctor to rule out health problems. Maybe a simple medication can be prescribed to help reduce the problem. Maybe you can remind your child to use the bathroom before bed. Maybe you can set an alarm to wake him in the middle of the night so he can use the bathroom when his bladder is full. In the meantime, it's probably a good idea to put rubber sheets on the bed.

By creating an action plan, you can do more than just hope the problem goes away, and you will also worry less about the problem because you're doing something about it.

59

Limit unhealthy choices

As a parent, I have to limit unhealthy choices for my child and me. Because I want us to live long, healthy and productive lives, I want to make sure we eat well, get our rest, get our exercise, fuel our brains and otherwise stay in shape for the long haul. It's important for me to be a good role model and for me to be around to raise my daughter, so doing my best to avoid a heart attack benefits my daughter as much as it does me.

In the same way, the martial artist who trains hard in class, going regularly, giving her best effort in every session and working to the point where her legs feel like spaghetti noodles doesn't want to spoil all that effort by stopping at a fast-food joint on the way home from training and scarfing down a double order of fries.

So she limits unhealthy choices. She knows that in order to be the best martial artist she can be, she needs to make wise choices—getting enough sleep, eating right, not overtraining, avoiding Friday night binges.

But unhealthy choices exist outside the cupboard door, too, and sometimes we don't recognize them as easily as we recognize the dangers of too many double cheeseburgers. My friend Helena's adult children seem to have benefited from her decision to toss the television. She advises other mothers to do the same "the day your first child is born." You can replace it, she says, only when you become desperate to get your kid's nose out of his book.

She handled complaints by letting her kids watch at their friends' houses and by working hard "to see there was good stuff happening at our house. I baked cookies, held Easter egg hunts, hung a hammock and in general tried to make our house a cool hangout."

My friend Carol wants her daughter, Kaeden, to have a healthy, balanced diet. She makes a special organic snack instead of feeding her daughter packaged animal crackers and similar snacks. She's careful to prepare meals with plenty of organic fruits and vegetables, whole grains, brown rice and the occasional free-range chicken. I suspect that Carol's husband has fed Kaeden a few French fries (I have no actual evidence) but the principle of this lesson is to *limit* unhealthy choices, not necessarily eliminate them entirely, and Carol has certainly done that.

Making healthy choices doesn't have to be a dull, dreary existence. Imagine how much fun it was to hang out at Helena's house! Much, much better than sitting in front of the television watching *Gilligan's Island* reruns.

Exercise

It's easier to limit unhealthy choices when your children are young and don't know better. Jessica has never thought it odd that we have no television, although if I had waited until she was seventeen to dump it, she would probably have had a strident objection. Even so, it's never too late to limit unhealthy choices. Start today with something important and find creative ways to make the healthy choice appealing. For example, if you and your kids don't get enough exercise, why not decide on a fun group activity that you can do together? The key is to get everyone to buy into the change and to support each other as you make the change into a habit.

60
Sometimes, remain silent

"I love my mother for all the times she said absolutely nothing," humor columnist Erma Bombeck once wrote. "Thinking back on it all, it must have been the most difficult part of mothering she ever had to do: knowing the outcome, yet feeling she had no right to keep me from charting my own path. I thank her for all her virtues, but mostly for never once having said, 'I told you so.'"

Martial artists learn that a lot of conflict could be avoided if people would just keep their mouths shut. Instead of escalating the tension or responding to provocation, if people just kept quiet, a lot fewer fists (and chairs, etc.) would fly. Sometimes we do have to speak up—we have to set boundaries, we have to let people know that we expect to be treated with courtesy and respect. But sometimes you can do wonders just by being quiet.

If we mothers can sometimes keep quiet, we let our children be themselves, discover for themselves. One of my friends describes a playgroup she brings her preschool daughter to. The children sometimes get into squabbles over who gets to play with what toy. But the mothers don't intervene immediately. They just keep having their conversation. Usually, the kids sort it out for themselves. They figure out whose turn it is, or decide to take turns, or one of them discovers an even more valuable toy she'd like to play with. But they wouldn't learn these strategies if the mothers kept coming over and saying, "Now, children, you have to learn to share."

Another friend tells the story of hearing her young son, mad at her, yell, "I hate you!" for the first time. So startled was she that she didn't say anything—she didn't reprimand him or try to empathize with him, she just didn't do anything. And after a moment he burst into tears and flung himself at her and said, "I love you, Mommy!" Well, no one said that children win the award for being consistent.

As a mother, I've tried to remember the importance of holding my tongue. Sometimes, when Jessica is pushing my buttons or pestering me, if I just keep quiet for a minute, good things happen. I don't make a rash promise that I can't or don't want to keep. I don't turn down a reasonable request just because my first impulse is to snap "No!" And instead of responding to Jessica pushing my buttons with irritation or exasperation—sometimes any attention is good attention—I'm silent and she stops pushing my buttons. Because nothing is happening. She pushes and pushes and nothing happens and that's boring so maybe it's time to go pester the dogs.

And sometimes, when she's talking and struggling to find the right word to say, I shut up and let her try to find it. Often she goes off in a completely different direction than I would have thought—that's why she's struggling to find the right words, it isn't the obvious thing she's trying to communicate to me. But if I start finishing her sentences for her, she gets hopelessly off track and confused, and I never get to hear what great connection she's made in her mind, or listen to the wonderful story she has to tell me about what happened at Grandma Kay's house last week.

And sometimes, when I'm not sure what to do next, I shut up and the answer comes to me. Give Jessica a hug, or take her and the dogs for a walk, or try a new approach or maybe—actually, a lot of the time—laugh.

So sometimes, silence.

Exercise

Try a moment of silence next time instead of falling back on your canned responses. Really think about what's needed. Is your child pushing your buttons? What should your reaction be? Does your child want something? What's the best answer you can give? Your first reaction might have been exasperation but very often your second reaction is just a rueful smile and the knowledge that you don't have to sweat it. You can just ignore it, and that's the best response for the situation.

61

Look in unexpected places

When martial artists reach a certain level of competency in their main style, they often set off to explore other styles. If they practice a striking style, they may gravitate toward a grappling style. If they train in a Japanese style, they may go find out what a Chinese style has to offer. They know this exploration of other styles helps them build their repertoire and become more effective martial artists. But they sometimes find the greatest benefit from looking in unexpected places. The founder of monkey-style kung fu incorporated the movements of a monkey to make the fighting techniques more effective. Who would have thought about basing a martial art on what a monkey does? Another martial artist went even further and incorporated the moves of a drunk person to create "drunken monkey" kung fu! The idea is that pretending to be drunk will throw your attacker off guard.

As a parent, you can also look in unexpected places for answers to your parenting challenges.

For example, I always tried to reassure Jessica when she felt anxious. ("It's going to be okay, honey, it's going to be okay.") That seemed like the compassionate thing to do. But sometimes that response only increased her anxiety. None of the child development specialists I consulted could help me. "Just keep reassuring her" was all they could say. Then I took a trick I learned from a veterinarian. When my dog Jasmine is anxious, I don't pet her and coo, "There, there, little puppy." As the vet explained to me, this just reinforces the dog's idea that there's something to be nervous about. If I respond with a firm, confident, "Easy, Jasmine, easy," then she feels calmer because someone's in charge (me) and I *sound* like I'm in charge. I stroke her with firm strokes instead of quick little pats, and she believes me.

So when being reassuring with Jessica only increases her anxiety, I tell her confidently, "You're doing great, no problem," and act straightforward and firm. Her anxiety disappears because I seem perfectly in charge and confident, and off she goes, eager to tackle what made her nervous just a minute before.

Yet for the most part I am still the mother who tries to respond with endless patience and compassion to my daughter. It's just that now and then another style is called for and works better. And sometimes the other style is the vet's.

Exercise

The next time your usual approach to a problem or concern doesn't seem to work, look in an unexpected place for answers. My gruff and brash know-it-all brother-in-law is a sucker for little kids. What a surprise when he could soothe Jessica with a pretend growl and big bear hug. Now I use the same approach when she's whiny. But he's not someone I would have thought to turn to for parenting advice.

On a trip to Washington, D.C., to film a TV segment, I had to bring Jessica along. It was spring break and none of the "family friendly" hotels had room. So I crossed my fingers and booked a room at a downtown business boutique hotel. And they fell over themselves catering to Jessica—calling her by name, bringing her chocolates, remembering what she liked for breakfast. The concierge arranged an excellent sitter and we had a delightful time. Perhaps because they rarely saw children, the staff had fun making a fuss over her.

So don't be daunted—use your creativity and look in unexpected places for answers to your challenges.

62
Smile

When I first began sparring, my instructor would have me go up against a partner and he'd watch for a little while, and then he'd say, "Are you having fun?"

Well, *fun* wasn't exactly the word for it. I was a little scared and a little intimidated. I was having trouble blocking all the kicks and punches coming my way. I felt inept and awkward. So, no, *fun* wasn't exactly how I'd describe the experience. But I was well trained, and so I would say, "Yes, sir!" and he would say, "Then smile when you spar."

This seemed like the silliest thing I had ever heard. I couldn't smile, I was too busy trying not to get punched. And even if I did smile, even if for some reason far beyond my current understanding, I one day wanted to smile while I was sparring, wouldn't that be defeating the whole purpose of the training? Wouldn't I be sending the wrong message to my opponent? That I wasn't tough, that I wasn't taking it seriously?

It took me a long time to see my instructor's point (I'm slow but I'm steady). It took me until I actually started having fun when I sparred. Then I realized that I didn't have to be so darned serious all the time. When you're having fun with friends in class, you don't have to be deadly grim all the time. It's fun to spar, so why not smile? So I started to smile in class when I sparred, to share the joy and to let people know I was having fun. It is not my fault that some people interpret it as "Ms. Lawler's evil smile."

When Jessica was first born, I was terrified that I'd screw up. The overwhelming knowledge that I was responsible for this fragile, tiny child made my stomach hurt. And at first having a baby wasn't very much fun. I had an enormous incision from the C-section, and it hurt, and my baby spent too much time in the ICU and I was scared. But pretty soon, I got it. I realized that having a baby didn't have to be so darned serious all the time. That it could be a lot of fun, and that you could smile.

I try to remember that I don't need to worry about all the little petty stuff—I need to just smile and enjoy Jessica. One day not so long ago, I was using my scolding-the-dogs voice, which is a deep tenor (they don't listen to my usual voice, I have to bark like a mama dog to get their attention) and Jessica started walking around the house imitating me. At first, I was a little irritated—it wasn't flattering and it seemed like she was making fun of me. Then she smiled at me. And I smiled back. And we had a good laugh. Now her favorite thing to do is go around the house using my scolding-the-dogs voice. Well, why not? It's funny, as I'm sure it struck her when she heard it that day. So it's always good for a smile. She uses it to charm me rather than to make fun of me. I'm glad I could see the difference.

Other times when she's hanging on my arm while I'm trying to talk to an editor on the phone or respond to an e-mail from a colleague, I'll just look at her and smile. She just wants my attention. I may feel like she's interrupting me and I have a lot to do, but isn't it nice that she wants my attention? Wouldn't I feel bad if she just ignored me all day long? Won't she be a teenager soon enough?

So I try to smile when I can, because it doesn't have to be serious all the time. It doesn't even have to be serious very often.

Exercise

Studies show that children laugh an average of 300 times a day. Adults laugh an average of five times a day. This is one area in which we could take our cues from our kids! Try not to take the role of mother so seriously. It's a lot of fun. If you can smile a few more times a day, you'll start to feel the joy and happiness of what you're doing a lot faster than if you're always frowning and serious about what's going on in your child's life and in your relationship with her. Add a couple more smiles a day, whenever you get a chance.

63

Take what you can use, discard the rest

Whether you're a martial artist or a mother (or both) who is exploring other styles (see Lesson #61), you'll come across techniques that don't work for you. As a martial artist, I'm sometimes shown self-defense techniques that would work fine if I were about six inches taller. But I'm not, so I don't bother with those techniques. Or, sometimes I'll be shown a technique that requires a lot of complicated fine motor skills, and I don't even try to memorize it because I know if I'm in the process of being mugged, remembering a forty-seven-step joint lock is not going to be within the realm of possibility.

On the other hand, sometimes I'll pick up a skill I had never been exposed to before, and I'll add it to my arsenal. At a martial arts workshop, for example, I learned some great breathing techniques that help stretch my shoulders and make me feel energized when I do them every morning. If I hadn't explored, I wouldn't have discovered this marvelous technique.

As a mother, I'm open to learning from other people. If a great idea worked for them, well, it just might work for me. But I also know that I can discard whatever information doesn't coincide with my values and beliefs, or simply doesn't work for me. For example, a homeschooling friend showed me how to use cooking a meal as a math lesson, so every time I so much as boil a cup of rice, Jessica is on her step stool beside me, counting and learning. But another friend, who sets a formal table every night, couldn't sell me on the idea that I needed to do the same. While Jess and I eat most of our meals together, often we do it while sitting at the coffee table in the living room. We still talk about the day's events, and we practice courteous behavior ("Please pass me the ketchup") but we're not formal. Maybe when Jessica is a little older, we'll find that having one or two formal meals a week helps cement lessons in etiquette, but for now it's not a technique we need.

Exercise

Just because everyone on the block does it doesn't mean you have to. Take what works for you and discard the rest—without feeling bad or guilty about it. Sure, maybe the other parents on the street spend every weekend carting the kids to soccer and band and volleyball and dance, but it's okay for you to limit each child to one activity. So pick the things that are most important to you, be open to other approaches and feel free to toss what doesn't work.

64
Focus on what you can do, not what you can't

As a parent, you'll need to focus on what you can do, not what you can't. Banish the concept of "I can't do this" from your vocabulary. Don't decide ahead of time that you can't send your child to a good private school or that you can't coach your daughter's volleyball team if that's what's important to you. If it's important to you, believe you can do it and work to find ways to make it happen. But don't start from the "I can't" position, or you can't.

This is a basic principle of self-defense: Focus on what you can do, not what you can't. If you're stranded on a deserted highway and your cell phone has died, you don't focus on the fact that you can't use your phone to dial 911; you figure out what you *can* do. If you're cornered in a dark alley and running away is not an option, then you can focus on the most effective way to stand and fight.

You can always do *something*. You'd like to be a stay-at-home mom, but the mortgage has to be paid. Instead of feeling sad, resentful and guilty about what you can't do, focus on what you can do. What aspects of being a stay-at-home mom appeal to you? Can you duplicate at least some of that experience? For instance, if one of the things you wish you could do was make gifts and bake cookies at holiday time, just like your mother did, then perhaps a simple solution would be to save your vacation time for the holiday season, rather than taking it in July. The key is to think about what you can do, using your intelligence and creativity.

When you work to banish "I can't" from your vocabulary (and your brain), and you focus instead on what you can do, you teach your children to transcend their own limits—in fact, they may never realize there are limits to what they can do, be, achieve. Wouldn't that be a wonderful thing?

Exercise

Don't assume that you can't do something. Always make sure you have the facts first. Start from the position of what you want to do, then determine how you can achieve it. For example, if you'd like your child to go to preschool in order to prepare for kindergarten, but you're sure you can't afford the enrollment fees, start from the position of power—focus on what you can do. First, find out how much the fees are. Perhaps they're lower than you expect. Perhaps there's a monthly payment option that would be easier to pay than a lump sum at the beginning of the school year. Maybe your community has a preschool co-op, where parents take turns helping out, thus keeping costs down. Maybe you can join with other parents in your neighborhood to create a preschool curriculum and take turns holding "class" in your homes. The important thing is to get the facts, and to focus on what you can do, not what you can't.

65
Speak another language

One of the many things I was unprepared for when I started training in the martial arts was that some of the instruction was given in Korean. Natural enough, I suppose, given that Tae Kwon Do is a Korean martial art. But there were times I thought I'd never memorize how to count—*hana, deul, set, net*—or do the correct kick when the instructor called, *"Ap chaki!"* Most martial arts are taught (at least partially) in the language of the culture that created them. It's an acknowledgment of, and a way for students to learn about and honor the culture that gave rise to the martial art. It serves to connect a far-flung group of people. If you practice Kenpo, then you'll be able to train with other Kenpo practitioners everywhere from Mobile, Alabama, to Inner Mongolia.

When Jessica was born, I had to learn another language. This was a medical one, which used cryptic abbreviations like SPECT and EEG and PRN, and words I'd never encountered before, like interictal and megacephaly, corpus callosum and astrocytoma, subependymal nodules and germline mosaicism. At first the words washed over me—I had no idea what they meant, I was intimidated by them, I didn't want to know what dreadful secrets they locked up. But it was important for me to understand what I was being told, so I could make informed decisions and figure out what to do next.

A friend of mine had to learn the language of special-needs education—IEP, IDEA, WIAT and WRAT; WISC-III, CAS, PCESE and KTEA; Woodcock-Johnson, Steinberg Triarchic and Stanford-Binet. And that was just the beginning. But by educating herself, she was able to understand not just what was being talked about or done, but the implications of these decisions—so that she could intervene if needed, question when appropriate and help direct her child's education. Since this language would follow her child in a record for the rest of her school years, it was important for her parents to understand its meanings and consequences.

But learning another language isn't just about being able to take care of your child appropriately. When another friend's young daughter started learning ballet, my friend had to learn to speak another language as well—one that included *arabesque, allongé, port de bras* and *tendu; pirouette, en face, jeté* and *plié.* By learning the language of a study that was important to her daughter, my friend was able to connect with her, understand what she was working on and happily discuss her daughter's progress with the instructor.

When we learn to speak another language, we can mediate between our children and the world, and we can connect with our children in ways we couldn't if we didn't know the difference between *temps levé* and *chassé.*

E x e r c i s e

Consider how much we could connect with each other and learn from each other if we were willing to speak another language. Instead of being intimidated by the idea of learning another language—whether it's the language of medicine or of geology—commit to it. You don't have to speak it like a native, but at least make the effort to understand some basics.

You can also take the principle literally and hire a tutor or rent language tapes from the library and learn a foreign language with your children. One of my friends told me the story of her young daughter who at age five became interested in learning Russian, the language of her grandmother. Her mother encouraged this by hiring an exchange student to tutor her daughter a few hours a week. She tried to pick up a few words herself so that she and her daughter could have basic conversations and she could reinforce the learning. Later, when they took a trip to Russia, my friend had enough words to function adequately (of the "I have a reservation" and "Where is the bathroom?" variety), and her young daughter was able to act as an interpreter, conveying lengthy, sophisticated conversations back and forth. Imagine how powerful that made her feel! And how delighted the Russians she encountered were to find this young American child able to converse with them. The skill gave the family the opportunity to enter into the lives of ordinary Russians, which they would never have otherwise had, and it gave these ordinary Russians a chance to get to know some ordinary Americans. Diplomacy at its highest levels.

66
Revel in your awkwardness as much as in your mastery

When Jessica's father and I first brought her home from the hospital, it became quickly apparent that we were not highly skilled. We used to call ourselves "the stupid parents" in order to acknowledge the fact that we didn't know what we were doing. But we would laugh over it instead of getting mad and upset with ourselves. We knew we'd eventually figure it out. And we did.

As martial artists, we both knew that being a new parent was just like being a beginning martial artist. A beginning martial artist is incompetent. It doesn't matter if she has been athletic before, she's still inept the first time she hits the mat. Learning the techniques and performing them correctly takes time and effort. Typically, the newby is a bit embarrassed by her awkwardness. Her glaring lack of skill makes her feel foolish. But why should it? Why would you be able to do the techniques of martial arts if you had never tried before? So instead of agonizing over the experience, why not enjoy it? That's one of the things I suggest to my students when they give me that rueful smile. Why not consciously experience the awkwardness? Why not laugh over how long you've inhabited your body without knowing it could do this?

When you bring your new child home from the hospital, or when your teenager enters that difficult moody stage, you're likely to feel awkward. How, exactly, do you get a diaper on a squirming two-day-old? How, in fact, do you discuss sexually transmitted diseases with your eleven-year-old? But enjoy your awkwardness. Experience it. Realize that if you rush through it, you'll be rushing through all the stages of your child's life. Smile when you hear yourself stutter. Appreciate that someday the awkwardness will disappear and you will become a more confident mother. Know that it will happen, but don't rush through the awkward stage just to get it over with. Think of how much you'll learn and grow. Appreciate the opportunity.

Exercise

Give yourself a break. You're not going to manage every parenting task with perfect aplomb. That's okay. Know that when you feel awkward and unsure, you're just going through a stage, too—and that you'll grow as a result of it. Kids survive all kinds of parental incompetence—they'll survive yours.

67

When you need to mother, abandon your worries

When a martial artist steps into the training hall, she stops worrying about what happened before she got there. She concentrates on what she has to do. She knows it's important for her to leave her cares behind because if she's distracted and unfocused, she's not going to perform well—and she might even get hurt. And just by jumping in and training, she's diverting her attention from the world outside the *dojo* to the world inside it. The more she makes a concentrated effort to leave behind her outside worries, the more the *dojo* becomes a place of committed training.

When we're dealing with our children, it's important to adopt this same mind-set. It's easy to feel like you're juggling so much that it's all you can do to get the kids dressed and on the bus to school, and feed them in the evening before packing them off to bed. But that's not the kind of relationship—or life—that any of us really want. So when you're dealing with your children, abandon your worries when you walk in the door.

Give your child at least so many minutes of undivided attention a day, when you're not talking to your partner, or answering the phone or responding to e-mails on the computer. When you're reading to your child before bed, be fully present. Don't be thinking about the report you have to finish before tomorrow morning. Either do the report or interact with your child; don't taint the interaction with worry.

Commit to distraction-free time with your children. Set aside a specific time, such as 7–8 p.m. Everything that needs to get done beforehand should be done beforehand. But when 7 p.m. rolls around, you abandon your worries. Whatever isn't done will have to wait. Spend this time consciously focused on your children. Eat a meal together, have a good discussion, play a board game. But give them your full attention, and don't be distracted by all the laundry that needs to be done or the vacuuming that hasn't yet taken place. It'll always be there—but your kids won't.

68
Build self-control

Mothers have to develop excellent self-control. They have to remember to think before they speak to their children, or they could hurt them far beyond how their words might hurt an adult. They need to count to ten instead of screaming when their four-year-old dumps milk all over the floor again.

Self-control is also one of the character traits that martial artists try to cultivate. "Self-control" has a couple of different meanings for the martial artist. It means physical self-control—practicing with your partners so that you're not kicking them as hard as you can. It means staying disciplined by training regularly and treating yourself right. It means controlling your emotions—not suppressing them or pretending they don't exist, but counting to ten when needed, thinking before speaking, de-escalating tension in a conflict.

We also need to teach self-control to our children. One of the smartest things I ever did was teach Jessica how to take a deep breath and relax. Whenever she'd get upset or confused or seemed ready to have a tantrum, I'd remind her to take a deep breath and get herself under control. Her preschool teachers thought this was a wonderful and amazing skill for such a young child to have. After a while, she would feel herself getting out of control and you could hear her take a deep breath and say, "Deep breath, Jessica. Deep breath." She learned to calm and soothe herself from a young age. Such self-calming skills will help her throughout her entire life. She learned the benefits of self-control when she was very little. We should all help our children understand and recognize these benefits.

By modeling good self-control, I'm able to help her learn it as well. If I pause, and take a deep breath before responding to her, she sees that this helps me remain calm and in control. If she sees me stop and enjoy a moment, she learns to enjoy a moment, too. If she sees me thinking before I respond, then she'll remember to think before she responds. Using self-control helps keep your relationships happier and your life on a more even keel.

Exercise

Help your child learn self-control by exhibiting it yourself. If you're screaming at the checkout clerk at the grocery store for being too slow, you can expect that your child will learn how to do that, too.

Use self-control to stop bad habits like that. In addition to modeling good self-control, give your child age-appropriate tools for slowing down, thinking about it, taking a calming breath. These self-calming, self-controlling techniques will be crucial for her in later life.

69

Act confident
and you will be confident

It's important for your children to see you appear confident and poised. They want you to be confident and sure. Yes, now and then you can admit you don't know where you're going and pull over and ask for directions. But if you act as if you're confident and strong, they will feel calmer and more confident themselves. They know that you can take care of whatever comes along, and that you will help them get through whatever difficulties they may face.

Martial artists know the value of acting confident. They know that if you're walking confidently down the street, you don't make a good target for a mugger or other criminal. He wants someone who will be easily frightened and intimidated. If you seem confident, he will choose another target.

The operative word here is "seem." You don't have to be fearless as long as you simply act fearless. The mugger will still avoid you, whether or not you're really confident, so long as you are projecting an image of confidence. And of course the more you act as if you are confident and sure of yourself, the more you become confident and sure of yourself.

When I started training in the martial arts, I realized the importance of projecting this image. By the time I had earned my black belt, it was no longer an image. I really was confident. I really did not feel afraid in most places. I knew I could handle myself, and I knew that I was smart about what I was doing and why.

You'll find the same holds true for your mothering. At first you'll have to pretend a confidence you don't feel. But over time, the confidence will become real. Of course, when your children grow older, they'll find out that you're not all-knowing and all-powerful. But when they're young, it's important for them to feel like you can handle anything, that you'll wrestle all the bears to a draw, kick all the wolves out of the campsite and banish the monsters under the bed. They need to have this belief in you.

If the floodwaters are rising and you let your kids know that you're panicked, you're going to have panicked kids on your hands, and that's not going to help matters. But if you seem calm and in control, you can lead them and show them what needs to be done. They are more likely to stay in control themselves and to follow your directions, making a difficult time much easier. It doesn't matter if you're panicked inside as long as you seem confident outside.

For example, most children tend to get anxious when they have to visit the doctor. Yucky things happen to children at the doctor's office, so who can blame them? But in my own experience, if I tell Jessica, matter-of-factly, that yes, she'll have to get a shot but it won't hurt very much, she'll manage to stay calm and face the music with courage. But if you're anxious about the visit, as I sometimes have been, chances are, your child will be even more anxious. Your job, as the adult, is to sometimes act confident even when you're not.

Indecision, anxiety, uncertainty—these are emotions you need to protect your child from as much as possible (in, of course, an age-appropriate way). Your child is not your confidante, and shouldn't be expected to bear adult burdens. So it's important for you to be willing to pretend you're confident even if you're not. If you can act confident even when you're not, you'll often find that you feel confident—able to face the challenges. And over time, you won't be acting anymore; you really will be calm and confident in the face of challenges.

70

A wise woman listens

A wise woman—a wise mother—listens. She listens to her children with her full attention, respecting their need to communicate. She listens to their ideas, and to their side of the story and to their descriptions of what is happening in their lives. She doesn't necessarily follow up with every idea or agree with every interpretation, but she listens, with her attention, compassion and empathy. And sometimes, as the Jewish proverb goes, a mother understands what her child does not say.

A wise martial artist also knows that listening is an important way to learn. If she listens to the instructions carefully, then she can follow them. If she listens to the instructor's feedback, then she can improve. By listening, she also builds her awareness of the world around her—her intuitive skills grow sharper. She knows that she won't always be able to see the instructor—sometimes he'll be in the back of the room barking out commands while she's facing the opposite way. By listening carefully, she'll be able to do as she's asked. And she knows that hearing the suggestions and corrections is as important as watching what others do and asking questions about the techniques.

When the wise mother listens, she teaches her children that they can come to her, that she will hear what they have to say and respect it and take it seriously. What a wonderful experience for a child when so often she's not accorded this respect. Since our children face many challenges in the outside world—from peer pressure to bullying to adults committing crimes against them—we need to listen to what they're saying and to what they're not saying. When they don't communicate with us, we shouldn't ignore it. We should try to find out why.

Exercise

Sometimes, just listen. Don't worry about what you're hearing. Don't think you have to parent every moment. Sometimes you just have to listen and nod your head. Don't think about what your response should be instead of actually listening to what your child is saying. And don't feel impatient, concentrating on how you don't have time right now. Just listen.

71

Bring only what you can carry

The martial artist keeps things streamlined. When she goes into battle, she doesn't load herself down. She brings only what she can carry—the spare, basic essentials. She doesn't bring several pairs of new shoes. She brings her sword and maybe a shield. When she trains, she brings herself and her commitment. She knows that extra baggage will only slow her down. She knows if she has to keep track of more than she can carry, she'll be distracted and unfocused.

When Jessica was born, I had a lot of baggage to haul around: all of my dreams and expectations, all of the dreams and expectations of other people, all the weight of what I should do and shouldn't do. It was very difficult to focus on what was important when I was distracted by what everyone else thought I should be doing. But when I began to streamline my expectations, I found mothering a lot easier—and a lot more enjoyable. I abandoned other people's dreams and expectations—I even abandoned my own. I promised myself I would deal with the present reality and not worry about the future or the past. Being able to unload extra emotional and mental baggage made me more effective as a parent. I stopped worrying about what to expect. I stopped comparing Jessica to other children her age. I just accepted her for who she was, and I lived each day as it came. I didn't dwell a lot on the future or the past. I just lived with the promise of today.

It was remarkably freeing to pare down what I was carrying to the bare essentials. My job was just to love Jessica, teach her what I could and guide her to becoming the best person possible. Other people's problems, worries, anxieties, thoughts and dreams for her (or for me) didn't matter. They were immaterial. They were not my problem. Shedding them made me feel lighter and more alive, more joyful in my parenting.

Set your own expectations—better yet, let your child set your expectations. Being a mother is a long journey, not a short sprint, and it's best not to haul a lot of unnecessary expectations along. Set the burden down. What other people want, expect or need is not your problem. Take only what you can carry—only what is basic and essential and eternal.

72

Believe in other people

As mothers, we should believe in other people. We can't be completely and solely responsible for our children learning what they need to learn to grow into happy and capable adults. By welcoming other people into our lives, we can expose our children to a variety of personalities, experiences, cultures and backgrounds.

A martial artist who tried to train on her own and who refused to let other people get involved wouldn't be much of a martial artist. Although martial arts is an individual enterprise—you're by yourself when you perform a *kata* (form)—you have a whole team behind you. Your teachers, your fellow students, other martial artists. If you don't understand that, or discount it, you don't stand much chance of becoming the martial artist you could be.

Apply this principle to your mothering, and you'll add extra dimensions to your child's life. My friend Helena, now a grandmother, says, "Try to have your adult friends to your house as often as possible, so your children can be surrounded by interesting adults." She remembers, "The very best thing about my own childhood was that we often had wonderful adults from many cultures around. I grew up hearing great gospel singing, learning from family friends how to do many kinds of crafts, riding a friend's horse and many other things all because my parents' friendships were wide and deep."

Claudia Bloom, the mother of a seven-year-old boy, echoes the importance of these types of relationships. "Help your child learn to be comfortable with other kids, with ones his age, younger or older and with adults—friends and relatives. We've included him in many social events and outings from the beginning—to visit friends/family out of the city for weekends away, to art openings, to kids' concerts, to weddings, to meals out with others. So many kids I know are not comfortable with many others, not sure how to hold a conversation with an adult, and I see the difference with ours very clearly."

By believing in the importance of other people in your child's life, you can enrich his childhood and give him opportunities to learn social skills that will help him throughout his life.

Exercise

Don't assume that just because you have a child, your adult social life is over. Find ways to have your children involved with the adults in your life. When you lunch with the ladies, invite your child to come along. When your child gets along well with other adults, and develops delightful friendships, it is a terrific confidence boost.

73

The angry mind forgets skill and discipline

I tell this story all the time because it demonstrates so well how anger clouds the mind and makes it difficult for you to act effectively. When I began training in Tae Kwon Do, there was a student who always, always kicked below the belt. He'd nail you in the thigh or the groin or in the knee. These are illegal target areas, meaning that you're not supposed to strike to them. In a tournament, you'd be disqualified. So this martial artist wasn't supposed to kick below the belt. He did it anyway. And it used to make his partners and opponents so mad, they couldn't spar him effectively. They'd just be yelling afterward, "He's not supposed to kick below the belt!" I saw this happen again and again. He'd line up to spar someone, and he'd kick the person in the thigh, and his partner would just go through the roof and would be completely ineffective for the match because he was so mad and frustrated. This situation was my first solid introduction to the fact that otherwise skilled and talented individuals could be reduced to frustrated impotence just because someone made them mad.

So whenever I sparred this guy, I knew he was going to kick below the belt. I just accepted that he was going to do it, and I didn't waste a lot of time and angst brooding about it. I saw him coming, and I did my best to spar him no matter what he did. And I could repeatedly score points on this guy and win matches with him when martial artists vastly superior to me in skill couldn't (or wouldn't) because they were so mad at him.

I applied this understanding to my own life. I realized that if I got angry and acted out of my anger, I wasn't going to be very effective or skillful at whatever I was doing. So I could feel my anger, and then just set it aside, and then act. I was more effective.

As a parent, I get angry over things all the time. I get angry over the way people treat my daughter. I get angry over the failings of the school system, which means I have to take on the burden of teaching my child myself. I get angry at the doctors who treat her like an interesting case instead of a little girl. I get angry at her when she pushes my buttons.

But if I acted out of all this anger, I wouldn't be a very good mother. Could you imagine? I'd be screaming at people instead of educating them about Jessica's disease. I'd be filing lawsuit after lawsuit against the schools instead of spending my energy teaching Jessica. I'd be storming out of doctors' offices instead of finding out how they can help me treat her problems. And I'd be yelling at her instead of figuring out why she's trying to get my attention. I'd much rather be the person acting effectively than the one acting out of anger.

All of us experience those moments of anger. When you've done everything you can to settle your baby and it's 2 a.m. and she's still screaming, sometimes you just want to scream, too. When your preschooler is called a nasty name at playgroup, you can feel your temperature boil. When your grade-schooler comes home from school and says, "A bully stole my lunch money," you're probably ready to march down to the bully's house and speak a few well-chosen words. But acting out of this anger makes you ineffective. Certainly you wouldn't want to take your anger out on your crying baby. And if you can calm down, you'll be likely to recognize that kids call each other names and it's probably not going to leave scars. And if you talk to your grade-schooler you may find out that he actually spent his lunch money on trading cards but didn't want to admit it to you. So taking a moment to calm down so that you can act out of a position of strength makes you a more effective, powerful parent.

Exercise

When you're angry, you forget what's important. You forget what your objective is. You just want to lash out. Instead, try to model good self-control. Just as you teach your children self-calming techniques, try some yourself.

Close your eyes, count to ten, ask yourself if it will matter in ten years. Sometimes if I'm honest I can see how ridiculous I look when I'm mad and then I start to laugh. I can do much more from a position of laughter than one of anger. Anger can certainly alert us to an injustice or a social ill that needs to be addressed. And acting to correct that injustice is right. But acting out of anger won't solve the problem. In fact, it interferes with your ability to act effectively.

74
Never cease to study

Sometimes we think we've earned our parenting knowledge and don't have to worry about acquiring more. We have a good relationship with our kids, and that's all that matters. But relationships change. Our children will grow, they'll have partners, they may have children of their own. And if you stopped studying—if you stopped growing as a parent—you'd have trouble dealing with these changes.

In the same way, some people attain their black belts and think they've mastered an art and don't need to study any further. They've missed the whole point of training. You don't master an art and then sit around and let it rust. You continue to study—to train—to maintain and improve your skills. If you earned a black belt ten years ago but haven't practiced a technique since, you're not really a black belt . . . you're someone who once earned a black belt. Only through continual training and study do you maintain your black-belt level. It doesn't have to always be the same kind of training or study. But it does have to be some type of study.

One thing I admire about my own mother is that she raised six children without losing her mind. My siblings and I constantly ask her advice about what we should do when the kid won't sleep through the night or he has a mysterious rash. And she'll share her wisdom.

But she also knows that knowledge changes over time and she doesn't have to be right. When she was raising children, for example, you put them to sleep on their stomachs.

That was the approved method. Now you put them to sleep on their backs, because studies show this reduces the incidence of sudden infant death syndrome. When Mom occasionally stepped in to watch our kids for us, and we'd ask her to make sure they napped on their backs, she did as we asked. She didn't pooh-pooh current research. She also didn't pooh-pooh us. She accepted that new information was worth paying attention to. Even when her own children were grown, she kept studying, she remained open to new information and to learning new things. We should all try to keep educating ourselves.

Exercise

Keep learning as a parent. Don't let hardening of the arteries (so to speak) prevent you from keeping up with current information and current studies. Don't decide that just because it worked for you a certain way it will work for everyone a certain way. And when it's time for you to spoil your own grandchildren, don't be so set in your ways that you can't listen to the new information that your children tell you about raising children.

75

Fear prevents joyful parenting

As mothers, we can feel like hostages to fate. We can be afraid of so many things. We can be afraid our children will get sick, or they will get hurt, or they will get hooked on drugs, or they will get pregnant at a young age. We can be afraid that they'll hang out with a rough crowd and drop out of school and start turning tricks on the corner. We can think of 900 things to fear, and that's just this morning.

When the martial artist trains, she isn't afraid of failing or about losing. When she trains, she isn't afraid of hurting herself or of stagnating or of never learning the technique. She knows that fear is not useful. It will just keep her from being the most effective martial artist she can be. It will just distract her from putting forth her best effort.

The martial artist knows that fear doesn't help. As mothers, we need to know this, too. Of course, we need to understand what the threats to our children are. And we need to take reasonable action. We need to give our children appropriate medical care, and we need to protect them as we can and we need to guide them so that they make healthy choices all their lives. And we have to know that if something bad does happen to them, we will do all we can to help them.

But being afraid isn't useful. It doesn't stop a bad thing from happening. But it can prevent you from truly experiencing the joys of parenting.

When Jessica was young, I was afraid that she would die. I felt myself putting her at arm's length because I was afraid of this. I didn't want to lose her, yet I was terrified I would. And that was no way to live. So I accepted that I might lose her. I wallowed in the pain of this possibility (I call it my "embracing the dragon" moment). And then I stopped worrying about it. Yes, it could happen. But my being afraid of it wouldn't alter the fact. My being afraid was interfering with our relationship. So I stopped being afraid.

I found that this was a useful skill in many cases. If I felt fearful, I did what I could to prevent the thing I was afraid of, and then I let go.

Instead of being too afraid to let your child go down the big slide at the park, do what you can to make sure she does it as safely as possible, then let her go. Instead of being afraid to let your child go to the pool with friends, give her swim lessons and then accompany them in a supervisory capacity. Once she's demonstrated that she can take care of herself (and if the pool has a lifeguard), then you can let go of your supervisory capacity. In other words, when your child is ready for you to take off the training wheels, don't let your own fears prevent you from doing so.

Exercise

Mothers worry. That's in the job description. But being afraid can affect your relationships, your health and your sense of calm and balance. So acknowledge that you're worried or afraid and make a conscious effort to put the fear aside. Reassure yourself that you're doing what needs to be done (you're buckling your kids in, you're teaching your preteens about drugs and sex) and let go of the fear. You'll find a lot more pleasure and joy in your parenting—and in your life.

76

The phoenix rises

Martial artists know that they can push themselves to their limits—and beyond—and feel utterly spent and physically and mentally drained and exhausted by hard training. They also know that with rest, they will wake up renewed and ready to try again. They may groan that they'll never be able to walk again, but they know that they'll be stronger because of the effort they put forth. If they don't tear down their muscles, the muscles won't grow back stronger. If they don't push themselves to develop physical, mental and emotional stamina, then they won't have it when it's needed. The martial artist pushes herself and rests and then, like the phoenix, rises again.

This is an important concept to remember as a mother. You can feel worn down and exhausted by the demands of mothering. You may have underestimated how tiring it would be to work full-time and care for a newborn. You can feel losses and grief. Your child won't turn out to be the perfect one you had envisioned. You won't be the Earth Mother you had thought you would be. You can see how your own dreams, desires and wants have to be delayed, given up, altered. You may feel the sacrifices are worth it, but you know there is a cost.

You can feel unprepared and overwhelmed. You can feel pushed to the absolute limit. Yet, with some rest and care, you will be able to get up again and face the demands of mothering. Be confident that this will happen. The phoenix is just as beautiful when it rises from the ashes! And you are the phoenix.

Exercise

The phoenix has many amazing qualities, not least of which is the ability to rise from the wreckage. If you're in a difficult, trying period now, remember that you are the phoenix and that you'll get through it and rise above it. Also recognize that if you're worn down and overwhelmed, you need the opportunity to rest and heal in order to rise again. Know that you grow stronger as a mother every single day.

77

Make play part of your everyday life

Play is an important part of learning. Children pick up many skills by playing games, playing with other children, playing with objects, exploring them, manipulating them. But as children grow into adults, they play less and less. Once we reach adulthood, we don't make play a priority. We don't think it teaches us anything, we think serious people don't play. Or we think that play is lazing in the sun on a Caribbean island.

Martial artists are serious about their training. They're committed to it, and they work hard at it. But sometimes they just play. They try to see who can kick the highest or who can throw the other person first, or who can spar the heavy bag longest. These moments of play can lighten the load and make the training experience more fun. The play teaches the martial artist something that she might not have learned otherwise in training. We used to play a game of tag in our school every now and then, using only certain kinds of kicks. Avoiding the people trying to tag you required different skills from sparring someone in the ring. And it was a lot of fun.

As mothers, it's important for us to play. We should play

ourselves—do things that we think are fun, like going to an adults-only cocktail party or hitting the ski slopes with friends. And we should also play with our children. It doesn't have to be traditional play, like playing a board game. It can be just an appreciation of how your child sees the world. Sharing a child's delight in the world is a simple form of play that makes you feel good. It reintroduces you to the wonders of the universe.

As my friend Helena says, "Most good parents instinctively understand that it's very helpful to make whatever has to be done fun. Walking with a small child is delightful because the world is new to them. A fire hydrant is a very interesting object until it becomes familiar." Helena played games when she wanted to speed up the slow process of walking with a little one, like "Catch My Shadow," in which she ran forward and the child ran to keep up, stepping on her shadow. Almost any activity can become play with a child, and almost any kind of play can be a learning experience for your child—and for you.

Exercise

You don't have to set aside special time to play with your children—although you can. Instead, try to find ways to play during ordinary days, doing ordinary things. Who can fold the laundry the fastest or clean up their room first?

78
Know what to do next

Mothers need to know what to do next. Being able to think ahead helps prevent you from making commitments, threats and promises that you can't or don't want to keep. And it helps you appear confident (See Lesson #69).

These are the exact reasons martial artists have to know what to do next. If they sense a potential threat, they may start with a nonphysical technique like saying, "I don't want to fight." Or they may try to walk away. They know that this may not be sufficient to stop the threat; and that they have to be prepared for what happens next. If they block a punch, they may have to punch the attacker themselves. If they kick the mugger in the groin, this may not be sufficient to dissuade the mugger, and they may have to hit him over the head. They know that there's no one secret technique that will solve all problems the first time it's used. What they have is the confidence that they know what to do next.

Two skills go into knowing what to do next. One is the ability to wait a moment and think before acting or reacting. That way if your child is pestering you for something, you don't say "Yes" just to get him to stop. And you don't say something like, "I'm never letting you borrow the car again!" when in fact you probably will. (Credibility is important for parents, too.) The other skill needed is the ability to plan ahead. If you know what result you want, and you have a handful of strategies for getting it, then you'll have a sense of what the next thing to do is. This is enormously comforting for children.

Suppose, for example, that your child is having trouble with a teacher and says the teacher "hates" him. This is probably not true, but it may require some investigation. Is it just a passing emotion because your child didn't do well on a spelling test, or is it a deeper problem? If so, what's your plan for dealing with it? If you decide to talk to the teacher but have no next step, what happens when talking to the teacher doesn't produce a satisfactory resolution? If you have a plan in mind, you can be calmer and more certain when you talk with the teacher.

Be open to changes—the teacher may have some ideas for dealing with the issue that you hadn't thought of—but also be willing to carry through and do the next thing on your list (convince your child to be more patient with her teacher, talk to the administrator, have conversations with other parents, transfer your child to a different classroom).

Knowing what to do next makes your children feel more confident, too. That's why you should create family plans for what to do in case of fire or tornado or a disaster occurring when you're separated during the day (where will you meet, who will you call, how can you signal that everyone is okay?).

Exercise

Instead of constantly reacting to what happens in your child's life (and your life), make a proactive plan. Decide what your steps should be. Know what to do next, whether it's dealing with the school bully or a child's sleeping problem. Think about the appropriate steps you should take. Be willing to change them if the facts say you should but at least have a general idea of how you'll deal with the various challenges that come along.

79

The master of the tea is a warrior, too

The tea ceremony is a ritual in which a tea master prepares tea according to specific rules using highly stylized movements. The ceremony helps the master and the participants open their minds to enlightenment and to achieve a state of calm detachment. This detached frame of mind was essential for the Samurai about to engage in battle. He participated in the tea ceremony, appreciating the ritual, understanding that he might not return. The tea ceremony is still highly regarded in Japan. The tea master studies for many years to learn the ritual, and is often a martial artist.

The master of the tea is a warrior, too. Not only because of her martial arts training, but also because the dedication, focus and training she undergoes to become a master is what makes her a warrior, whether she ever learns to draw a sword or not. Thus, the master of the tea, like the martial arts master, is worthy of respect.

As mothers, we often discount what we do. We think that anyone can do it and we also know that there are plenty of times we don't feel like we're doing the best job possible. But as long as we do it with love and compassion, then we are doing a good job. Treat yourself with respect, view your mothering role with respect and you'll receive more respect. Be confident that, like the master of the tea, you are capable and competent—that you are a warrior, too, even though you don't plan on drawing any swords.

Someone who doesn't know anything about Japanese culture would not realize that the master of the tea is a warrior, too. And so he might discount the tea master or think the Samurai was the more impressive person. But that's just an uneducated individual's perspective. Don't let other people's opinions affect your respect for yourself and for what you do. The master of the tea doesn't really care if no one knows she's a warrior. She knows it. She expresses it in all of her being. So only the truly uneducated would miss it and would mistake her for "just" someone who makes tea.

Exercise

Value what you do. One way to do this in a concrete manner is to keep an accomplishments list. This isn't about honors and awards, but it is about focusing on the positive. It isn't only or mostly about milestones ("Joey took his first step today"). It's about you as a mother honoring and respecting what you're doing.

So maybe you felt like you handled a conflict with your four-year-old effectively. Write about it in your accomplishment book. Maybe your five-year-old showed excellent table manners at Grandma's house. Congratulate yourself in the accomplishment book. Over time, it will help you see all the hard work you do put into raising your children and it will help you respect what you do. We tend to focus on what didn't get done or what we didn't do so well, but the truth is, we do a lot of really good things every single day and we should celebrate those things.

80

Don't always keep score

Sometimes martial artists get together and spar just for fun. No one keeps score, no one worries about who has more points. They just get together and have fun doing what they love to do. Not keeping score frees them to try techniques they would never do in an ordinary match. It allows them to set goofy rules, like "No using your hands." At the same time, these goofy rules can actually be good training. What if you have to fight someone when your arms are full? (Maybe you're holding your kid. Maybe your arm is broken and you can't use it.) If martial artists didn't sometimes let go and not keep score, they wouldn't feel so able to try new and interesting techniques. They wouldn't be open to seeing if something else could be effective.

Of course, some martial artists have difficulty letting go and not keeping track. They want to keep track no matter what. So they'll doggedly continue doing things the way they always have, taking everything seriously, deciding solemnly that they won the last match when you weren't even trying to fight traditionally—you were doing all your techniques from a handstand position.

As parents, it helps for us to lighten up now and then, too. It helps for us to not keep score. To just not worry about it. As Kathleen Winter, the mother of an adult daughter, says, "So often we waste time on petty stuff that we think reflects on us personally, such as a child misbehaving in the terrible-two stage when it's nothing more than a developmental phase." She says, "I sure wish I knew then what I know now!"—which is, don't worry about the little stuff. Don't keep score, don't keep track. Let the little stuff (and there is a lot of it) roll off your back. Concentrate your energy on the big, important stuff.

Exercise

As parents, one of the ways we keep score is by making a lot of rules and asking our children to abide by them. But it's worth stepping back and re-evaluating all those rules. Is it really important that no one eat cookies in the living room, or is it more important that everyone treat each other with respect? Is it appropriate to expect your two-year-old to display good manners or is it enough to keep her from killing herself? Focus on what's important and don't worry about the petty things.

81
If you think you don't have enough, you will never have enough

The martial arts are rooted in the Chinese philosophy of Taoism, and the book of Taoism, Tao te Ching, teaches us about the Tao (the Way). But our progress along the Way is often rudely interrupted or entirely derailed by distractions. One of these distractions is wanting.

The Tao te Ching tells us, "If you think you don't have enough, then you will never have enough." With the exception of someone who is homeless and starving, we all have enough. Most of us don't see it that way. Instead, we see what we lack. We think, if only we owned a bigger house or a fancier car, if our hair was blond or we weighed twenty pounds less . . . then, *then* we would be happy.

We do the same thing in our parenting. If our children were taller, smarter, more athletic. If they would just do their homework assignments or get a job, then everything would be fine. We want more for ourselves: If only we had more money or more time, we could be better parents. If our spouse was more supportive or our friends understood our situation, things would be so much better.

But if you focus on what's lacking, on what you don't have, then you will forget to see what you do have. And you will never have enough. There will never be enough money or time or energy. There will never be a tall-, smart- or athletic-enough child.

Instead, appreciate what you do have. Maybe you don't have a lot of money, but you're creative about stretching it, and you're teaching your children that money isn't everything—that love and self-respect are worth more. Maybe you don't have a lot of time, but you're committed to spending the time you do have with your children. They will appreciate that. As writer and mother Chris Strauss says, "You can make your children happy, you can make your children sad, but you can't make your children different. In other words, children come fully equipped with their personalities. You have to respect who they are and not try to make a thoughtful, quiet child into an outgoing student leader."

Focus on what you do have. In parenting, being positive is everything. Appreciate what your child can do, and celebrate your child's achievements, whatever they might be. Be glad that he or she has interests even though they might not be your interests. And appreciate that your circumstances give you "enough." You do have enough, if you just focus on the positive.

82

We're all teachers and we're all students

As a martial artist trains, she's expected to listen to and watch the instructor. She takes the role of the student. At the same time, she's expected to teach others. When she works with a partner, she's expected to give feedback or encouragement. She's supposed to teach her knowledge to people who are not as knowledgeable as she, even though she's not an instructor. She discovers that she is a teacher and she is a student, both at the same time. And both roles are rewarding. As she tries to explain to a new student why a technique is done a certain way, she learns a lot about the technique and about the martial art she's teaching.

As mothers, we can learn from our children as well. They can tell us what we need to know about them. And they can remind us of the important things. Rebecca Valentine, a columnist and "the mother of four and an angel" (as she puts it), remembers that when she was pregnant with her youngest daughter she learned this lesson well. Doctors told her that they suspected her baby might have Down syndrome. Since she and her partner did not intend to abort the child, she declined to have amniocentesis, which carries risks. So she and her partner gathered their children together to explain the situation. Max was eight, Tucker was four and Tavia was two. Here's how she tells the story:

> We gently explained to them that their sister might be born with a condition that would make her "different" from them. We gave a very basic definition of mental retardation and then we let this information sink in. Tucker broke the silence after a minute or two.
>
> "Can she pee?" he wanted to know.
>
> "Yep, she can pee," I said with a smile.
>
> "Can she laugh?" he asked.
>
> "Yeah, she'll be able to laugh," I assured him.
>
> Then with a satisfied grin and a shrug, he announced, "Then she won't be that different."
>
> Now it was my turn to let the information sink in. Tucker was right. I had gotten so swept up in the what-ifs that I had become blind to reality. It took a four-year-old to teach me what I once knew but had lately forgotten: It all depends on how you look at things.

A few months later, Rebecca's daughter Isabella was born without Down syndrome. But Rebecca will never forget what her son Tucker taught her.

Exercise

Don't forget that we can learn from our children. Be open to hearing what they have to say and to seeing the world through their eyes. Don't always think about what you have to teach them. Let them teach you now and then.

83

The relaxed mother is more effective than the tense one

When you're relaxed, you're much more able to deal with the challenges that come your way. You have more endurance for the difficult times. When you're tense, you can feel like you're trying hard but making no progress.

To be effective, martial artists have to learn this principle. Beginners never believe me when I tell them. They're always surprised to learn that the tense punch pushes against the bag with little power, compared to the relaxed punch, which snaps into the bag and whips it back. They usually have to try it ten times before they believe it's true. Keeping your muscles tense the whole time you're punching makes you very tired. You can't throw as many punches. If you keep your muscles relaxed, though, you have more endurance. You can be more effective. And your punches are more powerful.

In the same way, the relaxed mother can be more

powerful—and also more peaceful. Author and mother Phyllis McGinley writes, "God knows that a mother needs fortitude and courage and tolerance and flexibility and patience and firmness and nearly every other brave aspect of the human soul. But because I happen to be a parent of almost fiercely maternal nature, I also praise casualness. It seems to me the rarest of virtues. It is useful enough when children are small. It is important to the point of necessity when they are adolescents."

Your children can sense when you're feeling uptight and tense and they react to that (usually not in a good way). Think about it: The times when you're relaxed and feel able to handle the challenges of parenting, your children seem to push your buttons less, and even if they do come home with a terrible report card, you feel like you can work together to find a solution. But when you feel tense and stressed, something like a bad report card will set you off and instead of trying to find solutions, you end up getting mad, blaming everyone for incompetence and threatening your kid with dire consequences.

Exercise

Give yourself permission to relax. Realize that handling the challenges of parenting requires a calm, unruffled outlook. Do some stretching exercises, take a nap, soak in the tub—do whatever it takes to get relaxed and stay relaxed. The relaxed mother is much more effective than the tense one.

84

Commit to goals

The person who sets goals is more successful than the one who doesn't. Studies show that people who set goals and follow goal programs make twice as much money as people who don't—plus they're happier and get along better with their families.

The martial artist who strives to earn her black belt, who sees it in her mind's eye, who prepares for it, is more likely to achieve it. This is not to say that goals are the only purpose of training, or even the most important point, but they can certainly help you understand what you need to do to achieve mastery. If you don't have a goal to become a black belt, then will you commit to the necessary training? And if you don't commit to the necessary training, will you become as good a martial artist as you can be?

Just like the martial artist who has goals in order to stay the course, mothers should also recognize the importance of goals not only in their own lives but in the lives of their children as well. Mothers who set goals for themselves have children who tend to value goal-setting—knowing what they want and striving to achieve it.

When my sister Michelle returned to college to earn her teaching degree, her (then) pre-teen children watched her faithfully attend class and do her homework even when she was tired or not feeling well, and saw how she set priorities and reached her goal—while working and taking care of her family. Not only did this help them learn the value of goals, but they felt like all of them were in it together—taking classes, studying at night.

Exercise

Set some personal goals—things you'd like to achieve yourself. They don't have to be related to your children, but they can be goals that you share with your children so they can watch how you set about achieving them. My sister Bridget, for example, has the goal of finishing a novel that she has been working on. Her son actively contributes to her goal by helping her set aside time on the weekends and reminding her that she was going to work on her book on Saturday afternoon.

And set some family goals as well. Everyone can contribute. The goal can be something modest, like having dinner together at least twice a week, or it can be more substantial, like saving for a new house. The point is that everyone has to pitch in. Everyone has to arrange their schedule for those two nights a week. Everyone has to cut down on their favorite junk food to save for the new house.

With your kids, map out the goal and the action steps needed to get there. Ask for their help and cooperation. Showing them how to set and reach goals will be an important lesson for them later in life.

85

Patience

My mother says that patience is the most important quality a mother can have. Since she had six children of her own, I expect it was a skill she was called upon to use a lot. Imagine how many squabbles she had to referee and how many times she had to teach a little one how to tie shoelaces. If not for patience, she wouldn't have enjoyed the process—and we would not have learned as much or been as happy as children.

The martial artist must be patient, too. No matter how motivated you are, you cannot learn the techniques of a martial art in a weekend or even a week. Learning the techniques requires dedication, yes, but it also requires patience. It requires practicing a kick thousands of times before you know how to do it. It requires dealing with setbacks and plateaus. It means patiently building your muscles and your endurance. None of this can be accomplished quickly. But the patient martial artist is the one who eventually achieves what she wants to achieve, who becomes the best martial artist she can be. She doesn't get frustrated or give up when setbacks appear. She's patient. She sees it through.

As mothers, we have to be patient as our children learn new things and patient as they challenge us and patient as they grow up and sometimes need us and sometimes don't. Since most of us aren't born with quantities of patience, it's a skill we have to develop. Mom's suggestion is simple: "Just keep telling yourself, 'Patience is a virtue.'" In other words, you have to remind yourself that being patient is better for everyone in the long run. When you're frustrated, she says, ask yourself, "Does it really matter? Is it a big deal?" This can often take the weight off your shoulders. If you'll be five minutes late because of your toddler's dawdling ways, does it really matter? Maybe next time you can remember to start getting ready five minutes sooner.

Exercise

Practice patience. Remember that a sense of humor can help. My sister Bridget, who tends to be rarin' to go, knows she gets impatient when people are milling around instead of getting their coats and gloves on. So instead of getting impatient and yelling at everyone to hurry it up, she'll just shake her head and say, "We're off like a herd of turtles." It's a little reminder to herself that it doesn't really matter if it takes a few extra minutes to head out the door.

86
Effective mothers understand and accept themselves

When I say I was not athletic when I began training in martial arts, I mean I was not athletic. I was completely incompetent with my body. It was a wonder I could walk to class. Not only that, I hated my body. I'd had rheumatoid arthritis since I was nineteen, and the pain and stiffness discouraged me from doing very many active things. It will not surprise you that I was overweight and out of shape. I had just quit smoking. I thought I had a good brain, but my body I could do without.

But the very first martial arts class I took transformed my relationship with my body. Look at the things it was capable of doing! I was the merest beginner and already it could do things I never believed possible. The fact was, I was still overweight and out of shape. I still had rheumatoid arthritis. One week of classes didn't change that. But it did change how I saw myself. I had always underestimated what I could do because instead of accepting responsibility for my body, I hated it, I blamed it. I thought it was the enemy. So I treated it badly. Once I accepted that not only was I fat and out of shape, but that I was responsible for it, I began to understand why I treated my body the way I did. It always let me down, so I punished it. Knowing this was important for my being able to change. Accepting what I was helped me to understand why I was that way. And understanding my behavior helped me to change it. Once I saw what my body could do, that it didn't always let me down, I could take better care of it. I didn't have to abuse it with cigarettes and neglect. I could fuel it and exercise it and make it better and stronger.

What an important concept for me to understand. Of course it applies to my mothering, too. Like all of us, I want to be the best mother possible for my daughter. And I could pretend that I am always a fabulous mother, no matter what, every single day of the week, even at three o'clock in the morning. But that wouldn't be the truth. If I accept certain things about myself, I can understand myself and I can actually work to become a better mother.

For example, I know I work hard to be successful as a writer. I also know that I would give up just about everything and do just about anything to be a writer. I accept that I will jeopardize relationships, ignore people who need me and put my own wants and needs first when it comes to writing, because that's how I am. I accept that.

It doesn't mean that it's ideal behavior. But I accept that I'm a workaholic where my writing is concerned. This helps me to understand why I do some of the things I do. And it helps me to change. If I know that I'm a workaholic, then I don't accept my excuse that "I'll just finish this project and then I'll have more time to spend with Jessica." I know that when this project is finished, there will just be another one waiting in the wings. So I have to take steps to say, "I feel like if I finish this project then I can give Jessica all the time she needs. But I know I'll find some other project that needs to be done. So I need to step back from my work and give Jessica the time she needs now." If I didn't accept my workaholic tendency, I wouldn't understand it, and I wouldn't be able to take steps to balance it. By accepting yourself, you can understand yourself and make the changes that you need to make to be an effective parent.

Exercise

Accept who you are. Don't sugarcoat it. I'm not a hard worker; I'm a workaholic. There's a difference. It's okay. It is what it is. Unless you accept the truth about yourself, you can't understand why you do the things you do. And you can't make meaningful changes.

87

Clear mind, correct action

The warrior knows that if she is fearful or angry when she faces her opponent, her opponent has already won. This is because she won't make good decisions. She won't be logical and rational. A decision based on fear, doubt, confusion or anger can't be a good one. Before she engages in a fight or a conflict, she has to know what she wants to gain from it. What will she win? How will she win? If she can't answer those questions, she has no business acting. Yet often a person who is angry or upset feels compelled to act and does so without thinking—and therefore can't pursue a reasonable course of action.

When we make decisions about our children, we need to have clear minds so that we can take the correct action. One of the best ways to clear your mind when a difficult decision faces you is to meditate. You don't have to have any higher purpose when you meditate other than to clear your mind and calm down your emotions. And even if you don't have half an hour to meditate before making a decision, you can put some of the principles into practice—you can close your eyes, take some deep breaths, deliberately try to relax yourself and act out of clarity, not anger and confusion.

If you don't meditate regularly, it can take some practice. Pick a time when you can sit quietly, uninterrupted, for about half an hour. Go into a quiet, dark room and shut the door. Sit comfortably—a cushion on the floor is a good bet.

Close your eyes and focus on breathing in and out. Visualize an image or a thought or a word. It should be something totally neutral that doesn't arouse any feelings in you, except perhaps calm and peacefulness. I think of a candle flame. A friend of mine "listens" to the ocean. Focus on this image. Try not to let anything else enter your mind, just the image. (This is what takes practice! Our minds are a jumble of thoughts and ideas.) Concentrate on the image and on breathing slowly and deeply. When you feel calm and your mind seems clear, you're more able to make difficult decisions.

Exercise

The next time you're faced with a difficult decision and you have the opportunity to spend some time thinking about it, find a quiet place, away from bright lights and noise. Bring a journal into the room with you, meditate for a few minutes and then write about what is troubling you. This will help you find ways of responding to the challenge not based on fear or on the first reaction that comes to your mind.

88
The wise woman does what is right without speaking

The martial artist is expected to use her skills appropriately. That means that she doesn't attack people unprovoked. It means that she will try not to fight if she can help it. It means that she will protect other people who can't protect themselves. But she doesn't make a big, heroic production of it, taking ads out in the paper and proclaiming her righteousness. She does what is right, because she's a martial artist.

When the wise woman sees that she must act, she does so. Because she lives rightly, with integrity, her actions require little thought or justification. She just does them. She doesn't have to ask around to find out if she's doing the right thing. She knows she is. She's not worried about whether it will make her more popular or less popular. She knows what the right thing is, and she does it. If she needs to intervene in a fight, she does. If she needs to expose a crime, she does. She does not need to talk about what she's doing. She doesn't need to explain herself or get someone else's approval first. She knows she's responsible for right action.

A mother must also realize the importance of right action. She knows that she's a role model. She has children who look up to her. She must model the correct behavior for them. It isn't about drawing attention to what she's doing—"Look at me, see how generous I am!" Rather, it's about doing the right thing out of integrity and because she wants to teach her children to do the right thing.

Sometimes this is difficult because there is a personal cost. And sometimes you may not even like the people involved (you still have to do what's right). And often others—friends and family—may not support you. But you still have to do it. Even when it would be easier not to.

Exercise

Let your child see you do the right thing in all circumstances. She should see you treating other people respectfully, doing what you say you're going to do, telling the truth. Sometimes doing the right thing makes your kid mad at you—sticking to the usual bedtime no matter how much he begs, letting him choose only nutritious foods at the grocery store, siding with the teacher who gave him detention instead of trying to intervene or firmly sticking to the "No PG-rated movies" rule even though "everyone else" gets to see the newest action flick. You won't win any awards doing what is right—but you should still do it.

89
Commit to being
optimistic and positive

The Dalai Lama says, "Choose to be happy. It feels better." Or as my mother says, "If you make the best of it, your kids will go along with you." Making the best of it means being creative when money is tight or finding the edible parts of the burned chicken casserole. But children won't look on the positive side if you don't lead the way for them. If you look on the bright side, and you show them the bright side, they are likely to go along with you. If you look on the negative, dark side, they'll probably follow suit. You teach them this.

The martial artist is also expected to focus on the positive—she is supposed to be impervious to darkness and to fear. This means she tries to see the positive, the light, the good. And she tries not to be paralyzed by the negative, the darkness, the bad.

I remember during my youth we had a summer with a spate of tornadoes touching down in our area. The sirens would go off in the middle of the night and we'd all have to troop down to the basement and wait out the storm. We could have been terrified by this—and when I saw the tornado filmstrip at school, I was terrified. But Mom actually made it seem routine—and even kind of fun. She'd round us all up, spread us out on sofas and mattresses on the floor, bring a pot of coffee down and watch over us. There might be a fun snack or a game to play. She'd turn the radio on every half hour or so for an update, but she wouldn't keep it going constantly—she thought that might get on our nerves.

So I remember the summer, and I remember the nights spent in the basement, but I don't remember ever being afraid. Mom showed us how to take even a scary thing like a tornado warning and look on the bright side—it was like camping out, it was a change from the nightly routine, it was a chance for us to stay up a bit later than usual. But we wouldn't have responded so well if she had given into the fear or her worries about the storms, or if she had focused on the negative side of it—cranky kids in the morning, storm-battered garden, water leaking through the basement wall.

Exercise

Set the tone for your children. When you're on vacation and you land in a less-than-ideal hotel, instead of complaining about the accommodations, make the best of them. Anyone can complain. But it's a lot more fun to turn a less-than-ideal situation into an adventure. Focus on the adventure, not the negatives.

90
You are the *kata*, and the *kata* is beautiful

Traditional martial artists memorize patterns of techniques (the Japanese word is "*kata*"). *Kata* helps you perfect your technique, string techniques together, practice moving from one technique to another, perform techniques automatically (without too much thought) and improve your agility and balance. *Kata* requires effort and concentration.

The *kata* is beautiful. But the *kata* does not exist separate from the person who performs it. You are the *kata*. If the *kata* is beautiful, so are you.

Motherhood is a creative pursuit—like the musician making music, like the martial artist performing a form, you're intimately connected to what you've created. Being a mother allows you to connect with something larger, more universal, something outside yourself. In the moment of performance, transformation occurs. You are the *kata*, and the *kata* is beautiful.

Exercise

Know that your children—the result of your creativity—are beautiful even when sometimes they don't seem that way. And know that being a mother makes you beautiful, even when you don't feel particularly lovely and your hair needs to be brushed.

91
The centered Self reacts to few distractions

When the martial artist is performing a *kata,* that's all she's doing. She is centered in that moment and in that action. All of her attention is focused on what she is doing right now—performing a form.

Through her training, she learns to center herself in order to be ready for difficult tasks. She trains so that she won't be distracted by what's happening around her, but focuses on the goal or the task that's most important. She can use this ability to center herself outside the training hall. She focuses on what's important in her life, without worrying about unimportant distractions. At work, she chooses projects that must be done and does them. In her personal life, she spends time with her family and doesn't worry about the vacuuming that is still undone.

To achieve this type of focus, you have to be centered. You have to live a life of balance. And you have to say no. Sometimes we have to say no to our own children. But in order to say yes to our children as much as possible, we have to say no to other distractions. Why should these distractions—the annoying former friend, the telemarketer on the phone—get your attention when you need to spend some time soaking in a bubble bath or playing with the kids or taking the dogs for a walk?

Being centered means understanding that someone else's problem isn't necessarily your problem. People will try to hand you their problems but you have to resist the tendency to automatically make them your problem. This is especially true when our children want us to solve their problems for them. Yes, when they're two years old we may have to. But we have to give them the permission and the incentive to solve their own problems as they get older.

To stay centered and focused, it's important to know what your goals and priorities are. Concentrate on those goals. The more you focus the less scattered and stressed you feel. You know what you should do and you do it.

Exercise

Dedicate yourself to being centered. This means not letting yourself get pulled in fifteen different directions. Make an affirmation: I am a centered person. I am focused. Or any other phrase that you prefer. Pin it to the wall, tape it to your computer monitor, write it in lipstick on the mirror. Repeat the affirmation throughout the day, especially at those times when you feel competing demands on you. It will help you stay centered—and sane!

92
Don't look back
once the path is chosen

I always tell people that martial arts didn't change my life, martial arts *saved* my life. But I almost didn't let it. I knew from the minute I started taking lessons that I had found something good. I loved training. It made it possible for me to stay smoke-free. It helped me form new, healthy habits. I started losing weight and getting in shape. I felt more focused and disciplined outside of class—important because I was a graduate student going through a difficult patch in my studies.

I knew I was on the right path. I knew it. And I loved the person I was, and the person I was becoming. But for some reason—maybe because it's human nature—I kept looking back to my old life with longing. As if smoking three packs a day while sitting on the sofa reading was a life to be treasured. I didn't really want to be sitting on the sofa, but all the changes I had made were scary, and the thought of my former life was comforting.

I can't count the number of times I came close to hanging up my *dobok* (uniform)—not because I didn't like training or it was hard or I couldn't fit it into the schedule. It was just so darned difficult to give up my old life. I finally realized what I was doing, and I stopped looking back. I made an agreement with myself that if, after a year, the changes in me were too horrible to contemplate, I could always go back to the way I was. Suffice it to say I never did.

When you become a mother, it's easy to look back on the life you had before the baby came—when you got to sleep through the night, and you were able to eat a meal without interruption. When you could do crazy things like throw your backpack in the car and take off for points unknown. But if you look back too much, you'll resent the life you have. Your children will seem like a burden, a drudgery, something keeping you from what you want to be doing instead of making your life wonderful and full now.

In other words don't dwell on the fact that you were able to sleep eight hours straight before children. Concentrate on the present, focus on the here and now. Make a plan or two about the future, but don't look back.

Exercise

Live in the moment. Focus on what you're doing now. An occasional peek into the future is acceptable but not mandatory. Remind yourself of the downside of the life you had before. You may have been able to pack up and go, but did anyone care if you went? When I sometimes think I could get more done without my kid and the dogs, I remind myself that the kid and the dogs are the only reason I am where I am today—I wouldn't be a writer without them. Take care of today and tomorrow will take care of itself; take care of today, and don't dwell on yesterday.

93

Someone else's win is not always your loss

We're often jealous of other people's wins. It's as if we believe there are only so many "wins" to go around, and if someone else gets one, we've somehow lost. As mothers, we often fall into a competition of comparing how our children are doing. If yours learned to walk at ten months, then mine is not so wonderful, so special because she didn't learn to walk until later. If yours learned to read at four years old, then

I lose the competition if mine doesn't learn to read until she's six.

Martial artists view competition a little differently. Sure, they view it in a straightforward way: They either win or they lose. But the martial artist knows that when she trains, she will not always be able to defeat her partner. When she's a white belt learning the techniques, how will she learn them except by training with people who know more than she does, who are more skilled than she is? And because of that, isn't it likely that they will defeat her in their matches and she'll "lose"? But she wouldn't be able to learn to spar if she didn't do this.

She knows that fighting superior fighters makes her a better fighter. So if she loses a match but has improved her fighting skills, she hasn't "lost" anything. In fact, the loss would come if she agreed to spar only people with less knowledge and poorer skills. She would never learn and grow as a martial artist.

Of course, if you look at it that way, you can see that someone else's win isn't always your loss. As mothers, we need to stop the competition for the sake of our children. They develop at their own pace. We don't all share the same values and have the same gifts. I had to opt out of the competition very early in Jessica's life, or I would have gone nuts. For this reason, I didn't have much to do with mothers who had children Jessica's age. They didn't seem able to do much beyond compare their children. I stuck with friends who didn't have children or whose children were older. These people were more able to have perspective. They knew that just because Joey learned to read at age five didn't mean he'd be a National Merit Scholar when he graduated from high school. And even if he was, it didn't mean he was somehow "better" or more wonderful, delightful and worthwhile than the child who struggled all the way through school.

At the same time, I had to learn that other children could have wonderful accomplishments and I didn't have to discount them, or feel bad about them, or feel that Jessica and I had somehow lost.

When a friend's little girl started Montessori school and learned to read and write very quickly, even able to pen long reports about dinosaurs when she was just six years old, it was something I could enjoy. I could be happy for her and for her mother. It was wonderful that this little girl was so turned on by learning and could do so much at a young age. Her win is not my loss, or Jessica's loss. Jessica is not diminished by another child's successes. The only thing that matters is that she is nurtured and given the opportunity to create her own successes.

Exercise

Don't get caught up in the competition with other mothers. Deliberately step back from it. Instead of focusing on how old your child was when he learned to walk or when he said his first words—exciting milestones, to be sure, but not something to compete over—focus on other qualities. Talk about his sense of humor or how much fun it is to be a mom and see things through your child's eyes. Don't fall into the trap of comparing your child to others and thinking he's far superior or desperately behind. And when another child reaches an important milestone, be happy for him and for his mother. Don't feel that his "win" is a poor reflection on you or your child.

94

Practice Eight Directional awareness

Learning to trust your intuition (Lesson #41) and yourself (Lesson #56) means that you need to develop awareness of the world around you. The principle of Eight Directional awareness states that the attacker can come at you from one of eight directions (north, south, east, west, northwest, northeast, southwest or southeast). In other words, attackers can be all around you. They can even be above or below you. The most dangerous attackers are actually inside you.

That's why you should value awareness—awareness of the world around you as well as self-awareness. You should be aware of how you feel, mentally, emotionally and physically. You should develop your instincts because sometimes the attackers aren't in plain view.

Eight Directional awareness is not the same as paranoia. It is simply accepting, rationally, that threats to your well-being exist, whether physical, mental, emotional or spiritual, and you must be aware of them in order to take action against them. When your five-year-old hits other children whenever he gets frustrated, you can pretend you're not aware of it. Or you can dismiss it—little kids get frustrated and strike out. Or you can accept that being aware requires action. You can say, "You're not allowed to hit. You wouldn't like it if someone else hit you. We're going to go home now, and next time we come to playgroup, I don't want to see that behavior." Or, if you're slightly more laid-back, you can say, "Sweetie, please don't hit the other children. Why don't you tell Mama why you're mad."

Being aware of threats and acting on them helps you prevent more difficult challenges from cropping up. If you don't try to stop your five-year-old's inappropriate behavior while you can, it becomes harder to control and may even escalate into more inappropriate, unwanted behavior.

Exercise

Practice Eight Directional awareness in your relationships with other people. Make an effort to be more attentive. Pay attention to what your kids are saying and to what they're not saying. You should know the names of their friends, and the names of their teachers. You should know what their interests are, even if you don't share them. If you can't name your son's three favorite rap groups, you need to ask more questions and pay more attention. If your children know you're paying attention to them, they're less likely to seek attention elsewhere, or to settle for negative attention.

95

Visualize your performance

Because of my martial arts training, I believe in the power of visualization. So when I was pregnant, I used to visualize my labor and delivery going well. I would breathe correctly, focus on my chi, labor with little pain and produce a healthy baby girl in about an hour and a half. Of course, I actually ended up with prolonged labor, failure to progress and a C-section, but that does not stop me from believing in visualization. It served an important purpose—it significantly reduced my anxiety about labor and delivery. Worrying about that painful C-section before it happened wouldn't have lessened that pain after it happened. And I was able to enjoy my pregnancy more.

Martial artists know that in order to improve their performance, they have to obtain feedback from others. But they also have to set goals for themselves. They have to visualize, in their mind, what achieving their goals would look like. Often, after a training session, they'll take some time to do some meditation exercises that are designed to help them visualize what success looks like. They relax, and go over in their minds the training session just completed. They think about what they could have done differently—how they could have blocked that kick or how they could have performed the *kata* without a mistake.

Then they visualize themselves at their next training session (or their promotion test or a tournament). They visualize scoring all the points when they spar. They visualize nailing the *kata*. They feel how happy they are and how it looks to perform this way. Very often this imaginary effort helps them create concrete results—they see what happens and then it happens.

Often as parents we visualize the worst—our kid is late from school and we picture him in a ditch somewhere. But our minds and imaginations can also help us picture the best, too—our child is healthy and well, happy and pursuing meaningful work and loving relationships. If we focus on these good things that we want, we're more likely to attract them to our lives, and we'll think about how we can achieve them—

and we'll also see that we can't achieve these things for our children, they have to achieve them for themselves. So we can focus on what we can do for our children and let them take care of the rest.

Exercise

Visualize how you want your next interaction with your child to go. Maybe you have a difficult discussion coming up. Think about it ahead of time. What will you say? What might your child say? What would be a successful ending to you? Then try to approach the conversation with these goals in mind. Add details, textures, colors and sounds. The more real you make it, the more you'll feel confident that you can tackle the task. You'll be surprised at how this visualization prepares you for your parenting challenges.

96
Your breath gives you strength

Learning to harness your breathing gives you control over your emotions and helps you tap into your chi—your creative energy. Breathing correctly oxygenates your blood, which in turn gives you more physical energy. Therefore, breathing correctly when you exert yourself gives you endurance, which is why martial artists learn various breathing techniques to use when they train.

Breathing techniques can also be used to help you calm down and de-stress. The ability to reduce and control your stress level likes this helps you deal with challenges of all kinds, such as the fourth time this week your kid has spilled the pitcher of KoolAid all over the living room carpet. Martial artists (and other athletes) use many different kinds of breathing techniques, depending on their particular needs, but your basic goal should be to simply become conscious of your breathing.

Take a moment to be aware of how you breathe. Try to breath deeply so your chest and abdomen visibly expand. Then focus on expelling most (not all) of the air from your lungs to make way for a fresh intake of breath. Find a rhythm for your breathing. When you're stressed you tend to take shallow, uneven breaths. This doesn't give you the energy or the serenity you need to face difficulties. By deliberately taking deep, even breaths, you'll fool your body into thinking it's not stressed— and that's exactly what you need to cope with difficulties, the feeling that you're not stressed, and that you can handle this.

Exercise

Throughout the day, focus on how you're breathing. If you're sitting at the computer or fixing dinner, take a few moments to focus on deep, even breaths. Relax your face and your shoulders as you do this. Over time, you can eventually train yourself to breathe deeply and evenly on a more regular basis.

When you feel tense, practice simple focused breathing. Inhale deeply through your nose, filling your lungs to capacity. Then breathe slowly out through your mouth. Do this technique ten times, breathing in and out more slowly with each successive breath. You can also bring your arms out to the sides and pull your shoulder blades together to give your chest more room for expansion. Visualize the breath coming into your body as fresh and pure and expel the stress and negative energy. This breathing exercise relieves stress and can help you empty your mind and prepare for meditation or visualization.

97
Perform physical meditation

Martial artists often practice two different kinds of meditation, a quiet sitting meditation where you empty your mind or maybe visualize your performance, and an active, physical meditation. They know a state of transcendence and calm can occur during physical effort. Through *strenuous* physical effort, they can use their bodies and empty their minds at the same time, while finding the experience pleasurable. Think about the runner's high everyone used to talk about when everyone was running. It's a sort of hypnosis that releases all sorts of wonderful chemicals into your bloodstream.

You couldn't get the same feeling just from going for a nice walk (although a nice walk certainly has its benefits). Once you get into the rhythm of the physical effort, you stop thinking about how hard this physical effort is to sustain—and you feel energized and at peace. You're free to let your mind empty out. You don't really think about anything. You just work your body and you let your mind rest at peace.

Many of us spend our days sitting behind a computer or collapsed on the sofa watching television. Those of us with small children may be more active, but the activity does not lend itself to achieving transcendence. You're too focused on the main point, which is keeping your kid from killing herself.

By finding the time and space for physical meditation, you can use your body—work those muscles, get and stay in shape—and give yourself the chance to calm and clear your mind and de-stress from the demands of motherhood.

E x e r c i s e

Do a difficult activity for at least thirty minutes three times a week. Jogging, aerobics, biking, kickboxing—any of these physically demanding exercises will work (of course, always check with your doctor first before starting any fitness regimen). Focus on doing the movements correctly and on finding your rhythm.

Don't talk while you're exercising and don't use headphones. Ignore the distractions of others. Allow your mind to empty and to drift. Enjoy it. After some time (depending on your fitness level), you'll have to come back to earth and concentrate on your body again, but you'll still enjoy the feel of physical meditation afterward. You're more relaxed and less stressed.

98

If you don't fall down now and then, you're not trying hard enough

As mothers, it's important for us to accept that we'll make mistakes—we'll fall down. If we don't, it's probably because we're not trying hard enough, not because we're so perfect as parents.

Every martial artist who tries a new, difficult technique sometimes falls down. It's just the nature of martial arts. When you're supposed to spring into the air and do a complicated maneuver, sometimes you simply don't land right. You fall on your butt. That doesn't mean you shouldn't try the more difficult techniques. It just means you have to be fully prepared to fall on your butt.

People are afraid of falling down because they're embarrassed. Maybe they'll be laughed at. Everyone will be able to tell they're not a master, they're not perfect. But as a mother, you need to move beyond that concern. When Jessica was born, I tried to find the right balance of work and mothering. I wanted to have both in my life. And I ended up making a lot of mistakes trying to find the right balance. At first, I devoted time to my writing and found a day care center that would take Jessica part-time. That was a mistake. But I am nothing if not persistent. When the first center found Jessica's needs too difficult to deal with, I found another one. Same result. I suppose I could have guessed that such carefully regimented programs, strictly defined by age, wouldn't be flexible enough to take care of Jessica. Next I tried a home day care, thinking this would be more flexible, but after two days, the mom involved called me up and said, "This isn't working." Sigh. Another mistake. When Jessica began attending a special-needs preschool, I thought I'd go back to teaching part-time, since I'd have to be on campus for only about ten hours a week and I could schedule the hours for when she was in school. You guessed it. Another mistake. I hadn't counted on Jessica landing in the hospital three weeks after the semester started. So I ended up resigning the position halfway through the semester—not the sort of thing that is likely to result in glowing employee reviews. But I wanted to make it work. I was determined to make it work. And so I finally found the right combination of sitters and activities and working nights and weekends so that I could do all that I wanted to do.

Falling down as a mother just means that you're trying to have high expectations for yourself and your children. And there's nothing wrong with that. But don't beat yourself up when you land on your butt. Learn what you can and keep trying.

Exercise

Be willing to fall on your butt. Be willing to up the ante. Have high expectations for yourself and your kid. When you fail, at least you're closer to your goal than if you'd never tried. If you think your kids are too young for something, think about giving it a try anyway. If you think you're not skilled enough, try it anyway. You might be pleasantly surprised.

99

Kiss the owie, move along

You direct your children. As long as you don't act like something is a big deal, then your kids won't think it's a big deal. Most new mothers learn this lesson when their babies are learning to walk. If the baby falls down and the mother says, "AWK! Oh, no! My baby fell down!" the baby is going to take the cue and start to cry. Most of us soon realize that if you just bite your tongue, the baby will fall down, look surprised, get up and try again. The baby won't even realize that she should cry. Little ones this age look to their mothers to learn how to react. If they trip and fall or pinch a finger, they look to see what they should do. If mama seems calm and unworried, then the child doesn't worry about it.

A martial artist knows she's going fall down now and then (see Lesson #98) and that it's going to hurt—her elbow, her pride, her sense of herself. But she also knows that people are resilient and she needs to get up and get moving. If she stays on the floor, staring at the ceiling and feeling sorry for herself, she'll never master the jump spinning wheel kick. So she acknowledges the pain of the mistake and she gets up and tries again.

This is a skill we should pass along to our children. Accept the hurt—kiss the boo-boo—and move along. If toddlers dwelled on how they fell down the last time they took a step, they'd never take another. And if mothers remembered how tough labor and delivery was, everyone would have only-child families. So acknowledge the pain of the mistake, learn what you can from the experience and go on.

Exercise

My friends on the Freelance Success online forums have a saying, "Eat a cookie. Move along." They use the mantra whenever they get a rejection letter or have to deal with a nasty editor or client. And it's valuable advice. A cookie or an ice-cream cone, or *Monsters, Inc.* on DVD can take help console you or your child. Then move along.

100
Love

If you do nothing else as a mother but love your children completely and wholeheartedly, you'll have done enough. Remember that no amount of "quality" time or toys or attention will make up for lack of love. So enjoy your children, take pride in watching them grow—but most of all, love them and open your heart to their love.

My sister Beth says, "People tell you how much you'll love your baby, but when you actually hold that child in your arms you realize you never knew or felt anything like it before in your life. It's inexplicable—the total and overwhelming love where you know you would lay down your life for that person. That you would do anything to take away any hurt—but that you can't always do that. It's like your heart is on the outside."

I will never forget that after years of medical problems and scares and difficulties with Jessica, one day, when she was about three and a half years old, I was tucking her in bed and she looked up at me and said drowsily, for the first time ever: "Love you, Mama." I would have given my life for that moment. It made everything worthwhile. And if I never hear another good thing in my life, that will have been enough.

Exercise

Love your children, and let them love you. Wear your heart on the outside.

Conclusion

Jessica and I have just started our adventure together. She is now seven years old and we have, I hope, many more years to come. I know that if I'm wise and remember the lessons of the martial arts, I will delight in watching her grow and seeing her become a young woman I can be proud of. The experience may not be the same for me as it will be for another mother, but all of us can rise to the challenges and accept the promises of motherhood by remaining open to the path. I hope that you are able to look on your mothering journey as an adventure, too, one that may be filled with challenges to overcome but exhilarating and joyful nonetheless.

When I began writing this book, I had to sift through hundreds of pieces of advice from mothers, stories they told about what had worked and what hadn't—and why. I had to fit the pieces into the *Dojo Wisdom* framework. If I wanted to illustrate the point, "Teach the consequences," I had to find someone who had done this and could give an example or an anecdote about how they had used it in their own lives. In the end, so much information didn't make it into the book, because it either repeated something already said or didn't quite work in the context in which I wanted to use it, that I think I may have to persuade my publisher to let me write *Dojo Wisdom for Mothers II: The Sequel.*

Some of the quotes that didn't make it in were barbed comments: author Quentin Crisp saying, "My mother protected me from the world and my father threatened me with it," and poet James Fenton commenting, "The lullaby is the spell whereby the mother attempts to transform herself back from ogre to saint." Some were a bit cynical: journalist Mary Kay Blakely saying, "'Mother' is the first word that occurs to politicians and columnists and popes when they raise the question, 'Why isn't life turning out the way we want it?'" Some were thoughtful: Erma Bombeck saying, "Mothers are not the nameless, faceless stereotypes who appear once a year on a greeting card with their virtues set to prose, but women who have been dealt a hand for life and play each card one at a time the best way they know how. No mother is all good or all bad, all laughing or all serious, all loving or all angry. Ambivalence rushes through their veins." Some were sentimental: the Danish proverb someone forwarded to me: "Who takes the child by the hand takes the mother by the heart." And others not so much: the anonymous mother who commented, "Fall out of the nest already, you guys, will you? It's time."

The number and diverse nature of these quotes captures the dilemma of the mother—her role is ever-changing and is viewed—and judged—from many perspectives. But as I hope *Dojo Wisdom for Mothers* has shown, what matters is that you become the mother you were meant to be, learning from others yet striking out on your own: In other words, take what you can use and discard the rest.

There was one piece of advice that although I couldn't quite fit it into the overall puzzle, I felt deserved to be Lesson #101. It comes from my very wise sister Beth and applies to all mothers everywhere: "Sleep when you can. And carry Handi Wipes."

Pilsung!

Dojo Wisdom

In the hours spent perfecting their skills in the *dojo*, martial artists practice much more than how to master a punch. They also learn essential lessons that help them become stronger, calmer, and more courageous people—and enhance their lives. In *Dojo Wisdom*, Jennifer Lawler, a martial arts teacher and second-degree black belt, shares 100 of these life lessons from the martial arts to help anyone find his or her inner warrior. Each lesson begins with a descripton and explanation, and also offers a short exercise to illustrate how to apply the teaching in everyday situations. This accessible, encouraging, and inspiring book can show you—whether or not you ever step onto the mat—how to tap into a power you never knew you had.   ISBN 0-14-219622-3

Dojo Wisdom for Writers

In *Dojo Wisdom for Writers*, Lawler shares 100 essential lessons from the martial arts that she used to build her own career and that will help aspiring writers everywhere. Inspiring, wise, and always down-to-earth, *Dojo Wisdom for Writers* is a valuable addition to any writer's library. ISBN 0-14-219631-2

FOR THE BEST IN PAPERBACKS, LOOK FOR THE

In every corner of the world, on every subject under the sun, Penguin represents quality and variety—the very best in publishing today.

For complete information about books available from Penguin—including Penguin Classics, Penguin Compass, and Puffins—and how to order them, write to us at the appropriate address below. Please note that for copyright reasons the selection of books varies from country to country.

In the United States: Please write to *Penguin Group (USA), P.O. Box 12289 Dept. B, Newark, New Jersey 07101-5289* or call 1-800-788-6262.

In the United Kingdom: Please write to *Dept. EP, Penguin Books Ltd, Bath Road, Harmondsworth, West Drayton, Middlesex UB7 0DA.*

In Canada: Please write to *Penguin Books Canada Ltd, 10 Alcorn Avenue, Suite 300, Toronto, Ontario M4V 3B2.*

In Australia: Please write to *Penguin Books Australia Ltd, P.O. Box 257, Ringwood, Victoria 3134.*

In New Zealand: Please write to *Penguin Books (NZ) Ltd, Private Bag 102902, North Shore Mail Centre, Auckland 10.*

In India: Please write to *Penguin Books India Pvt Ltd, 11 Panchsheel Shopping Centre, Panchsheel Park, New Delhi 110 017.*

In the Netherlands: Please write to *Penguin Books Netherlands bv, Postbus 3507, NL-1001 AH Amsterdam.*

In Germany: Please write to *Penguin Books Deutschland GmbH, Metzlerstrasse 26, 60594 Frankfurt am Main.*

In Spain: Please write to *Penguin Books S. A., Bravo Murillo 19, 1° B, 28015 Madrid.*

In Italy: Please write to *Penguin Italia s.r.l., Via Benedetto Croce 2, 20094 Corsico, Milano.*

In France: Please write to *Penguin France, Le Carré Wilson, 62 rue Benjamin Baillaud, 31500 Toulouse.*

In Japan: Please write to *Penguin Books Japan Ltd, Kaneko Building, 2-3-25 Koraku, Bunkyo-Ku, Tokyo 112.*

In South Africa: Please write to *Penguin Books South Africa (Pty) Ltd, Private Bag X14, Parkview, 2122 Johannesburg.*